An Alternative Take
on the Great White North

Geordie Telfer

© 2010 by Folklore Publishing Ltd.
First printed in 2010 10 9 8 7 6 5 4 3 2 1
Printed in Canada

The Publisher: Folklore Publishing Ltd.
Website: www.folklorepublishing.com

Library and Archives Canada Cataloguing in Publication

Telfer, Geordie
My Canada : an irreverent take on Canada's past / Geordie Telfer.
Includes bibliographical references.

ISBN 978-1-894864-81-7

    1. Canada—History—Humor. I. Title.

FC173.T44 2010   971.002'07   C2009-906392-1

Project Director: Faye Boer
Project Editor: Kathy van Denderen
Illustrator: Djordje Todorovic
Cover Image: Images courtesy of Dynamic Graphics (Mountie); iStockphoto: ©Carsten Madsen I iStockphoto.com (tin soldiers); Photos.com (maple leaf, snow).
Photo Credits: Every effort has been made to accurately credit the sources of the images. Any errors or omissions should be directed to the publisher for changes in future editions. *Images courtesy of: The Bookman: A Magazine of Literature and Life,* August 1902 (p. 252); Cathy Ord (author photo, p. 352); *Chambers's Encyclopaedia.* William & Robert Chambers, Limited, ©1899. (pp. 10, 26, 42, 47, 92, 176, 187, 189, 250, 251, 333); Geordie Telfer (pp. 162, 288); *The Illustrated London Geography* by Joseph Guy, ©1852 (p. 121—Franklin Engraving only); Library and Archives Canada / Reproduction, C-078979 (p. 170), PA-091061 (p. 194); Roberts & Co. mail flyer, Vancouver, BC, July 1928 (p. 341); *The Strand Magazine,* July to December, 1892. Illustrated Interviews No. XVI. (p. 204).

We acknowledge the support of the Alberta Foundation for the Arts for our publishing program.

We acknowledge the financial support of the Government of Canada through the Book Publishing Industry Development Program (BPIDP) for our publishing activities.

Dedication

For Valin,
who makes history in his own way

Contents

Introduction

IF STUDYING HISTORY HAS taught us anything, it's that half of the events we think happened may have never happened at all, and if they did, probably didn't happen the way we think. This book is an attempt to provide some balance by looking at real historical events from perspectives that are not merely skewed, but in most cases, at a 90° angle to reality.

For instance, what if the Hudson's Bay Company monopoly on the fur trade had been played out as somthing like a game of Monopoly? What if there had been Top Ten Lists when Henry Hudson was cast adrift in 1611? What if there had been reality TV when Canada was settling the question of Representation by Population? And what if, rather than focusing on the movers and the shakers, we looked instead at the supporting players—the forgotten voyageurs, the unnamed lumberjacks, the men who sold the Fathers of Confederation their hats?

All of the larger historical events described in this book did take place, but here you will find them viewed from a different, and at times, subversive point of view.

Enjoy this book, and stay skeptical.

–Geordie Telfer
Toronto, 2009

ONE

Putting the *Inuk* in *Inukshuk*

Now famous as Inuit symbols of welcome, inukshuks are markers constructed of stacked stones. They are thought to have originated as offerings to propitiate the gods in hopes of good hunting. On a purely secular level, inukshuks may have served to mark the migratory routes of caribou in a landscape devoid of trees and other landmarks. The next time you're sitting around a fire waiting for a herd of caribou, you can try telling the following tall tale to fill in the gaps.

Semerssuaq and Kakuarshuk

THERE WERE TWO SISTERS NAMED Semerssuaq and Kakuarshuk. Semerssuaq was the older one and refused to marry because she could find no man who was her equal in either mind or spirit. Kakuarshuk was the younger one who didn't mind the idea of marriage but nor did she flit here and there feverishly seeking a mate like so many do. Semerssuaq and Kakuarshuk were each complete on their own, but nonetheless they were very close as sisters.

A man named Akigsiak was the best soapstone carver for miles around. When people praised his carvings, he would say, "You just have to carve from the inside out. There's a shape waiting in every piece of soapstone, and all you have to do is let it out." Kakuarshuk found this to be an admirable point of view, and even Semerssuaq had to admit that Akigsiak's way of carving soapstone was an attractive one.

One day, Akigsiak asked Kakuarshuk to be his wife and she accepted. Then Akigsiak asked Semerssuaq if she would like to come and live with them. Semerssuaq said yes, since otherwise she would miss her sister. Also, she did not mind Akigsiak's company because he was always carving a piece of soapstone and did not really say much. So when Kakuarshuk and Akigsiak were married, Semerssuaq went to live with them, and all three set off for the winter hunting grounds.

Akigsiak was a very good soapstone carver, but beyond that he was very lazy. Besides, no one was around to trade soapstone carvings with, so it was a pretty useless thing for him to be doing all the time anyway. Semerssuaq was an excellent hunter though, so the family did not starve. After Semerssuaq gutted the carcasses, Kakuarshuk would scrape them clean with her *ooloo*[1] and make

[1] An all-purpose knife with a bone handle and a wedge-shaped metal blade; the curved outer edge of the blade is sharpened for cutting and scraping.

clothes and other useful things out of them. Eventually the sisters grew tired of Akigsiak's lazy ways and the ever-growing collection of soapstone carvings they had to cart around with them.

"Aja! Where were you when they were handing out the testicles?" Semerssuaq asked. "It is outrageous that you expect Kakuarshuk and I to do all of the work while you sit there and make soapstone dust! You call yourself a man?"

"Life is like a soapstone carving," said Akigsiak. "There is a shape waiting to emerge, and I am waiting to see what that shape will be." Although they were still frustrated, Semerssuaq and Kakuarshuk had to admit that Akigsiak did seem to be practising what he preached. They could not argue with that.

The winter continued, and Semerssuaq was pleased to find that there was excellent hunting and fishing in the area they lived in. She made sure to thank Sedna[2] every time the hunt was successful, which was often. Semerssuaq tried to think of some way to mark these fertile hunting grounds so that both her family and others could find them again in the future. Perhaps if she made some sort of offering to Sedna, it would assure Sedna's continued favour? But although her mind was quick like a hare and strong like a bear, no ideas in this regard came to her. Finally, Kakuarshuk suggested

[2]An Inuit sea goddess

The village of Semerssuaq and Kakuarshuk before their departure to live with Akigsiak. Opponents of the seal hunt did not exist yet, but if they had, they would have died from starvation in short order.

⎯⎯∿∿∿⎯⎯

that Semerssuaq should take Akigsiak's advice and simply wait to see what shape emerged.

When the time came for them to break camp and move on, for once, they made Akigsiak carry all of his own carvings. Kakuarshuk gave him one of the sealskin sacks she had made, and the two sisters watched as he loaded his soapstone carvings into the bag.

"You know," said Kakuarshuk to Semerssuaq, "it's as though the purpose of his life is missing, and all that's left is the shape of a man."

"Well," said Semerssuaq, "you're the one who married him."

"Thanks for reminding me," said Kakuarshuk.

Akigsiak slung the heavy bag over his shoulder, walked out onto the ice and fell right through! He scrambled out again and made it back to land, where he started stomping his feet and waving his arms to warm up, but it was too late—Akigsiak froze solid with both feet on the ground and his arms outstretched. Semerssuaq and Kakuarshuk raised their eyebrows when this happened for they had never seen anyone freeze solid before.

"Perhaps it is a sign from Sedna," suggested Kakuarshuk.

"You are right," said Semerssuaq. "She is showing us the way to mark our hunting grounds."

"And perhaps it is also the way we can make an offering or sacrifice to her."

"Akigsiak is not much of a sacrifice," said Semerssuaq. "And besides, we cannot drag a useless man around with us wherever we go in the hopes that he will freeze solid whenever we find good hunting and fishing grounds."

"You are right," said Kakuarshuk. "We would have to feed him, too."

"But what does occur to me," said Semerssuaq, "is that we could stack stones in the shape of a man to mark our hunting grounds and as an offering to Sedna."

"Aja! But you are a clever one, sister! The stone figures will serve as guides in this land devoid of trees or other landmarks, and the work of stacking the stones will be our offering to Sedna."

"Exactly."

"What shall we call these stone figures?" asked Semerssuaq.

"Well, you yourself said that Akigsiak was so lacking in usefulness that he was merely the shape of a man, and yet now, here he is, frozen and dead, finally serving a purpose worthy of a man, namely, acting as our guide to these fine hunting and fishing grounds."

"And the stone figures will do the same."

"Exactly. So I would suggest that we take the word for man—*inuk*—and tack on something that means 'substitute.' What do you think?"

"Perhaps *shuk*—*inukshuk*. Yes, I like it."

Semerssuaq and Kakuarshuk moved on to new hunting grounds and lived long lives. Eventually, Kakuarshuk took up with a new man who was not useless. Semerssuaq went to live with the new couple, and the three of them enjoyed many evenings around the fire, singing into each other's throats and laughing over the day's adventures. But wherever the hunting was good, they stacked stones to show the way to others and to thank Sedna for the bounty she provided.

An inukshuk in the shape of a person

And that is how the *inukshuk* came to be.

WHAT'S REAL

Like everything else in this book, the narrative itself is completely fabricated, but the general tone was informed by written versions of oral legends from both Greenland and Labrador that are listed in the sources for this chapter.

Inukshuk means "serving in the capacity of a man," but it can apply to any sort of pile of stones used as a marker, even simple cairns that are not shaped like people. The kind of inukshuk made in the form of a person with outstretched arms is properly called an inunnguaq, meaning "imitation of a person."

I did not find any tales, stories or legends that seemed to provide an explanation of the inukshuk origin, but there is almost certainly one out there.

TWO

So-called Potlatching

Of all the First Nations traditions that pre-date the arrival of the Europeans, one of the most famous is the "potlatch," so-called by the white men hundreds of years later. In this section we take a friendly look at those brief windows into Canadian history that have themselves become part of our late 20th-century cultural landscape—Heritage Minutes. For those of you who don't know, Heritage Minutes are short, inter- stitial pieces about 60 seconds long that air on TV and radio, celebrating moments from Canadian history, often in highly idealized form.

HERITAGE MCMOMENT #1

```
FROM: Richard Wanker
Broadcast Executive
Historical TV Channel

TO: Mordant Wit
Freelance Writer

Hi Mordant,
    I'm so glad you've signed on as our
writer for the Heritage McMoments series
```

☞

(we think the "Mc" is a nice nod to
the Scottish heritage shared by so many
Canadians and in no way sounds like
a fast-food breakfast sandwich). I just
wanted to give you some background
on the series—the idea is that we
will produce one-minute vignettes that
celebrate Canada's history, then supply
them free to other broadcasters to
help them meet their CanCon quotas
(every little bit helps). We hope to celebrate all aspects of Canada's history.

I'm a bit of a writer myself (at
least, I've given notes to a lot of
writers), and so I've taken the liberty
of drafting up something to show you
what we have in mind. I know that visuals would normally go in the left-hand
column, but I've sort of glossed over
that (I leave that sort of thing up to
you), and then I realized that I'd typed
all the dialogue in the left-hand column anyway, and I couldn't be bothered
to change it. I thought you could make
whatever notes you have in the right-
hand column, but I don't expect there
will be many :)

Looking forward to your feedback,
Richard (Dick) Wanker

Heritage McMoment #1:
The Tradition of the Potlatch

Suggestions for visuals: We could maybe see a bunch of Indians—sorry, *First Nations* peoples—standing around a roaring fire and giving stuff to each other—you know, stuff like beads and so forth.

NARRATOR	WRITER'S NOTES
Long before white men came to Canada, there was an ancient tradition of sharing among Canada's First Nations peoples.	*OK, well, the first problem is that they most likely would have given each other food or something a bit more practical than beads, and the tradition was prominent in the Pacific Northwest, not all over Canada.*
CHIEF My people believe in sharing with one another. *(Chief gives some beads to someone else.)*	*See note, above, regarding beads.*
CHIEF It is a strict law that bids us to distribute our property among our friends and neighbours. It is a good law. Let the white man observe his law; we shall observe ours. *(Chief nods sagely to the camera.)*	*Your quote about the "strict law" appears to have been lifted straight off Wikipedia where it is attributed to Chief O'waxalagalis of the Kwagu't who lived into the 20th century, well after the arrival of white men.*

☞

CHIEF
We call this tradition the potlatch.

OK, look, the word "potlatch" comes from Chinook Jargon that traders made popular from the middle of the 1800s to the beginning of the 1900s—no chief would have ever called it this, especially before the arrival of the Europeans.

You conveniently avoid mentioning that the white man outlawed potlatching because it was an impediment to making good Christians out of the Indians—another sad example of the brutal oppression that makes up so much of Canada's history. Perhaps we could do a History McMoment about brutal repression?

NARRATOR
The potlatch—the redistribution of wealth—was an important idea in Canada even then.

FROM: Richard Wanker
Broadcast Executive
Historical TV Channel

TO: Mordant Wit
Freelance Writer

Hi Mordant,
    So glad that you liked the draft script I sent—not to toot my own horn, but I'm pretty pleased with it. ;)
    Looking forward to working with you on the next Heritage McMoment: "Peter Pond Discovers the Alberta Tar Sands."

Sincerely,
Richard (Dick) Wanker

WHAT'S REAL

Potlatching, of course, was a real tradition and was banned in 1885. The word "potlatch" comes from Chinook Jargon as described in the "Writer's Notes" column. Chief O'waxalagalis was a real person, and the statement in the script beginning "It is a strict law..." is attributed to him.

THREE

The Norse in Newfoundland

John Cabot and Christopher Columbus were not the first Europeans to visit North America. Archaeological evidence suggests that sometime around 1000 AD, a small community of Vikings settled in Newfoundland in the area currently known as L'Anse aux Meadows. What follows could have been their story.

The Land of the Long Days
(A Saga of the Discovery of Vinland)

THIS IS THE SAGA OF THORKEL Thorkelson, whose father was also called Thorkel Thorkelson, their forebears not being smote by the gods with imagination. Thorkel Thorkelson the Younger had quite a temper, but this did not prevent him from becoming one of Iceland's most successful farmers. One day, Thorkel Thorkelson's friend, Snorri Snorrison, came to Thorkel Thorkelson's house to borrow his handsome box made of hand-carved Mosuki wood.[3]

"Snorri Snorrison," said Thorkel Thorkelson, "you know that box is a family heirloom. Leif Eirikson himself gave it to my grandfather (who was also

---

[3]Likely maple

called Thorkel Thorkelson) after Leif Eirikson came back from his adventures in Vinland."

"I don't believe there is any Vinland," snapped Snorri Snorrison.

"Yes, there is!" thundered Thorkel Thorkelson. "It is across the ocean. You hang a left at Greenland."

"There is nothing to the left of Greenland," said Snorri Snorrison.

"If you were not my friend, I would tear your arms from their very sockets for disagreeing with me!"

"Be that as it may, would you consent to lend me your box?"

"Sure thing," said Thorkel Thorkelson, "but be sure you give it back."

"Sure thing," said Snorri Snorrison.

And so Snorri Snorrison went home with Thorkel Thorkelson's handsome box of hand-carved Mosuki wood, which Thorkel Thorkelson's grandfather (also called Thorkel Thorkelson) had been given by Leif Eirikson when Leif Eirikson returned from Vinland (which Snorri Snorrison did not believe existed anyway). Snorri Snorrison's reason for borrowing the box was not a very noble one; he wanted to use it as a footrest when he sat in his house at night snoring off a bellyful of spruce beer in front of the blazing fire pit. One night, Snorri

Snorrison's wife, Gudrid the Broadminded, came out from the bedroom to fetch him. She shook his shoulder, whereupon he jerked awake and accidentally kicked Thorkel Thorkelson's box of hand-carved Mosuki wood into the fire.

"I shall come to bed at once, Gudrid," he said for, Viking though he was, Snorri was sensitive to (and indeed, eager to fully satisfy) Gudrid's desire to have a little Viking. They went into the bedroom, and all thought of the soot-blackened box that he had accidentally kicked into the fire vanished from his mind.

However, Thorkel Thorkelson's wooden box came rapidly back into Snorri Snorrison's mind when Thorkel Thorkelson knocked on his door the following spring and testily demanded its return. Snorri Snorrison, suddenly realizing that he had kicked the box into the fire one night before an amorous interlude with Gudrid, hurriedly said, "Why the rush? You only live three fjords over; I'll just bring it by on Thor's Day."

"I am impatient and I have quite a temper," roared Thorkel Thorkelson. But then he said quite amiably, "So let's make it a day sooner on Woden's Day."

But that Woden's day, instead of returning the wooden box (which was now ashes anyway), Snorri Snorrison left Thorkel Thorkelson a hastily carved rune stone that said, "Sorry, but I accidentally kicked your Mosuki wood box into the fire. It is ashes now. Yours truly, Snorri 'Sorry'-son."

Upon reading Snorri's ill-advised play on words, Thorkel Thorkelson flew into a rage and killed his entire village (except for the immediate members of his household as well as Snorri Snorrison and Gudrid who were away in the north hunting reindeer). Thorkel was promptly banished from Iceland's shores forever and quickly announced his intention to sail immediately in search Vinland and, once there, to find Mosuki wood for a new box.

Thorkel Thorkelson collected his wife and cattle. His wife was called Aud the Awful. The cattle were called Ingrid, Helga, Dottirson and Sven (the bull). However, on the way to the ship, Aud the Awful slipped and fell into a volcano that happened to be erupting just then. All of the onlookers felt that this was a bad omen, but Thorkel Thorkelson felt that it was, on the contrary, quite a good omen. He immediately asked his maid of all work, Thurid the Deepchested, to accompany him in his search for Vinland and to run the household he would surely build there. She blushingly accepted.

Along with some Viking friends from neighbouring villages, Thorkel Thorkelson and Thurid the Deepchested set sail for Vinland. After many days of wild seas, they found themselves looking at a vast shore that stretched as far as the eye could see. Thorkel Thorkelson spied grapes growing on vines along the shore and said, "We shall suppose that this place is Vinland, on account of the grapes and vines growing here. But what do I want with grapes? It is the Mosuki tree that I want so that I can make a handsome new box of hand-carved wood. We shall sail farther north in search of wooded lands."

And so the ship and her crew sailed on for many days until they arrived at another vast shore, this one covered in slabs of rock—desolate and still. "Because this place is full of slabs of rock, we shall call it Helluland.[4] But what do I want with rocks when it is trees that I am after? We shall sail back to the south." And so Thorkel Thorkelson and his crew (many of whom were getting pretty tired of booting all over the ocean) sailed south again until they came to a shore that was heavily forested. Thorkel Thorkelson was very excited about the trees. "We shall call this place Markland,[5] and here we shall make our home," said Thorkel Thorkelson. And so they did.

Meanwhile, back in Iceland, Snorri Snorrison and Gudrid the Broadminded returned from their reindeer-hunting trip with many fine carcasses. Gudrid was particularly excited about the antlers because she wanted to make a pair of bone knitting needles to knit baby booties, since she was now

---

[4]Helluland means "Slabland." They may have seen Baffin Island.
[5]"Mark" means "forest"—"Forestland"; possibly Labrador

happily with child. When they returned to their village and saw that everyone was dead, Snorri Snorrison said, "I am afraid that Thorkel Thorkelson has done this in a fit of rage because I accidentally kicked his wooden box into the fire. I shall sail after him to apologize properly." So Snorri Snorrison and Gudrid the Broadminded summoned some sailors from a village the next fjord over and set sail.

In Markland, Thorkel Thorkelson was well satisfied that Thurid the Deepchested had consented to make the journey with him. As the maid of all work at his farmstead in Iceland, Thurid the Deepchested had learned what a household needs to run smoothly. She had brought with her many useful housewares: several stone oil lamps, a whetstone for sharpening blades and many other practical items of Scandinavian design.

One day, while Thorkel Thorkelson was outside setting up a blacksmithing forge, several men with high cheekbones and red skin[6] emerged from the woods. They were almost naked.

"They are almost naked," said Thorkel Thorkelson. "For this reason I shall call them Skraelings."[7]

"Look at how frightened they are of the cattle," said Thurid—and indeed, all of the Skraelings were starting to back away from the cattle with a slow

[6]Possibly either Mi'kmaq or Beothuk people
[7]Wretches

hesitant sort of wandering step. Then the Skraelings went to their boats, clambered in and paddled away.

"They must never have seen cattle before," said Thorkel Thorkelson.

Over the winter, Thorkel Thorkelson's settlement found the going easy. The winter was cold, but not as cold as in Iceland, and even the shortest day of the year had longer hours of sunlight than at home. Best of all, Thorkel had found an ample supply of Mosuki trees and was industriously carving himself a new box.

The leaves of the Mosuki tree sought by Thorkel Thorkelson. Speakers of ancient Norse may notice a striking resemblance to the leaves of the common maple (*Acer campestre*), since adopted as the emblem of Canada.

But as the weather warmed and the days grew longer, Thorkel noticed Thurid looking at him in an odd way. Finally, one evening while he was putting the final touches on his hand-carved box, she approached and said, "Thorkel Thorkelson, when you asked me to come to Vinland with you to run your household, I had thought—indeed I had dared to hope—that you might be looking for more than a maid of all work."

"Ah…" said Thorkel nervously. "Er…well…"

The truth of the matter was that Thorkel Thorkelson was not what we might nowadays call a "people person." In truth, he was something of a psychopath with homicidal tendencies, which made him a poor mate but a good Viking. Being emotionally unequipped for an honest relationship, Thorkel decided it would probably be easiest to simply give in to Thurid's wishes.

"Er…" he repeated in a not very Vikingly way. "Of course, Thurid. Um…let me give you this… uh…" He looked about their humbly furnished sod house trying to find some token of his presumed affections to give to her. Finding nothing, he unclasped the bronze fastening pin that held his cloak on and pinned it to Thurid's cloak. She beamed at him and kissed him on the cheek.

"Oh, Thorkel, you have made me so happy!"

By the time the first buds appeared on the trees though, Thurid's happiness was melting like the

winter ice, leaving a large puddle of lukewarm sen-
timent in its place. She realized that Thorkel
Thorkelson, though he was handsome in a brutish
sort of way, was about as personable as a slab of
granite. However, she was now pleased to be with
child, Thorkel having managed to demonstrate at
least one human reflex, albeit a largely involun-
tary one.

For his part, Thorkel had completed his wooden
chest and was now harvesting a shipload of lumber
to take to Greenland where wood was a valuable
commodity. Soon there was a fine harvest of logs
neatly stacked on the shore. Tired from cutting
down all the trees, the people in the small settlement took a holiday, and everyone decamped to
the surrounding area for picnics and so forth. Even
Thorkel went, convinced by Thurid that they
needed some time away together.

As the fates would have it, on the very day that
the village was abandoned for the holiday, who
should drop anchor off the shore but Snorri
Snorrison, Gudrid the Broadminded and their
shipload of sailors from Iceland. Seeing an empty
village with a cargo of valuable logs neatly stacked
and waiting for transport, Snorri lost no time in
loading them onto his ship, at which point Thorkel,
Thurid and the entire village arrived home again.

Thorkel, seeing his wood loaded on to a strange
ship and then seeing none other than Snorri
Snorrison standing by with a pleased look up on

his face, flew into an homicidal rage. Indeed, Thorkel had raised his sword to smite Snorri a mighty blow, when the Skraelings suddenly attacked. If Thorkel had not given his bronze fastening pin to Thurid, then he might have been wearing his cloak and the Skraeling arrow might have been deflected. But as it was, the arrow struck Thorkel Thorkelson in the armpit, killing him instantly. The villagers and even Snorri Snorrison were inclined to view this as a bad omen, but Thurid the Deepchested felt that it was, on the contrary, quite a good omen. They dragged Thorkel's body into the house. Once they were inside, the body of Thorkel Thorkelson sat bolt upright! Snorri, who happened to be standing nearby, leapt back in fright.

"By Thor's hammer," he gasped, "what is this?!"

"It's the *aptrganga*,[8] said Gudrid. "*Aptrganga* happens all the time in the ancient sagas. Have you never heard of it before?"

"No," said Snorri. "What happens now?"

"I will tell you some fragment of foreseen knowledge or useful lore," said the late Thorkel testily.

"Well, make it quick," said Snorri.

"If the Skraelings have never seen cattle before, then it stands to reason that they've never had

[8]The temporary and usually brief return to life of a corpse—a common belief in ancient Iceland

milk before," said Thorkel Thorkelson. "Why don't you go out and see if they want some milk? Maybe they'll trade you some furs for a bit of milk instead of destroying the settlement."

"Alright," said Snorri. "Which one of you is going to go out and offer the attacking Skraelings some milk?"

"I'm pregnant!" said Thurid.

"As am I!" said Gudrid.

"And I'm dead," said Thorkel rather unnecessarily.

"So?" said Snorri.

"You would endanger not only your wife but also your unborn child in this way?!" shouted Gudrid. "What kind of Viking are you?"

"A cowardly one," said Snorri.

"Fine!" said Gudrid and went out with a bowl of milk to offer the attacking Skraelings. To everyone's surprise, after tasting the milk, the Skraelings halted their attack and paddled away to return the next day with furs, which they left in exchange for more milk. Things went on quite amicably this way until autumn rolled around and the grass started to shrivel up for the winter. Without the juicy grass to eat, Ingrid, Helga and Dottirson could not produce as much milk, and the Skraelings grew restive.

"You realize you've gotten them hooked on milk, don't you?" said Gudrid to Snorri one day.

"Well, you're the one who went out and offered it to them," said Snorri, who was only spared the indignity of being murdered by his wife at this point because the Skraelings chose this moment to attack once more.

"Run away!" said Snorri as he led the rest of the settlers in fleeing the village. But Thurid and Gudrid could not run as fast as the others, both being great with child. After stumbling along behind the others, the two women had had enough and, caring not whether they lived or died, turned to the advancing Skraelings, tore off their shirts and slapped their bare bosoms with the broad sides of their swords. It was done more in frustration than defiance, but the Skraelings were greatly frightened by this and turned around and ran back to their boats. Thurid and Gudrid returned to the village for a nice drink of milk.

Gudrid and Thurid decided that they had had enough of this New World and told Snorri in no uncertain terms that the time had come for them to return to Iceland. Snorri and the rest of the villagers agreed. By this time, Thorkel Thorkelson's body had fallen to pieces, and his widow packed the bits neatly into the hand-carved box he had made so they could take him back home—Thorkel Thorkelson had gotten his new box at last.

The little fleet set sail once more, its ships laden with furs, precious lumber and a dead man in a box. The day after they set sail, Gudrid gave birth to a little girl they named Gudrid Gudridsdottir. Snorri Snorrison was rather glad there would not be any more Snorri Snorrisons for he had always thought it quite a silly name. As they sailed past Greenland, they saw a pod of sea unicorns[9] frolicking in the waves, and everyone was inclined to view this as a good omen. When they saw the shores of Iceland creep over the horizon, Thurid gave birth to a little boy who was called Thorkel Thorkelson.

Thorkel Thorkelson's father had also been called Thorkel Thorkelson.

WHAT'S REAL

The foregoing fake saga was adapted from two real sagas that chronicle the Norse discovery of North America (Vinland) by Leif Ericson, whose father, Eric the Red, discovered Greenland. While the names have been changed for entertainment purposes, many of the events are taken directly out of the original texts: Eric the Red and his father, Thorvald Asvaldson, had to leave Norway because of "some killings"; Eric was involved in a disagreement

☞

[9]Narwhals

over some wooden bench boards that had not been returned to him; "Mosuki" is a Norse word that does appear in the original saga and was used as a catch-all term for many different kinds of trees, including maple; the Norse travellers landed at several spots up and down the coast of North America (any present-day place names mentioned are those thought by scholars to be possible landing sites); the Norse settlers brought cattle with them, much to the consternation of the Aboriginal peoples they encountered (likely Mi'kmaq or Beothuk); Vikings, though they were men, seemed to have had little compunction in sending women into dangerous situations, such as bribing possibly hostile Skraelings with their first taste of milk; valuable loads of lumber were harvested and taken to Greenland; and the sagas do mention dead people coming back to life with useful information.

Finally, among the items unearthed from the Norse settlement at L'Anse aux Meadows were bone knitting needles, stone lamps, a whetstone, a bronze fastening pin, as well as the remains of an iron smithy and a woodshop.

FOUR

Early Explorers of Canada

The year 1967 marked Canada's centennial. From coast to coast, new buildings, parks, films, plays and books were all falling under the banner of "Centennial Projects." What better time to explore Canada's rich heritage? What follows is one such project that probably never got off the ground.

(From the records of the Maple Leaf Novelty Company)

February 12, 1967

FROM: Earnest Patriot
Freelance Illustrator

TO: Milton Scheister
President, Maple Leaf Novelty Company

Dear Mr. Scheister:
   I would like to present you with an idea that I think could make us both extremely wealthy. As you know, Canada's centennial falls on July 1, now just

☞

a few months away. In these months leading up to that date, centennial-mania has already begun to sweep the country. What better time to introduce a line of trading cards glorifying the early explorers of Canada?

Please find enclosed a few sample cards that I have taken the liberty of creating: they celebrate John Cabot, Jacques Cartier and Samuel de Champlain. I realize that all of their names start with "C," but I think that this makes it extra patriotic, since Canada starts with a "C" too.

As regards the obligatory stick of razor-sharp dried bubblegum we will be expected to insert into every pack, why not stamp them out in the shape of maple leaves? This would give the gum several extra pointy corners to further lacerate the gums of anyone foolish enough to actually chew it.

Sincerely,
Earnest Patriot

JACQUES CARTIER
Explored Canada:
1534, 1535, 1541

Nationality:
French

JACQUES CARTIER
Stats:

1534
- Claims Gaspé Peninsula for France; Iroquois First Nations dismayed
- Kidnaps Chief Donnacona's two sons and takes them back to France

1535
- At the Iroquois settlement Hochelaga, names nearby hill "Mont Royal"
- Survives scurvy with help of Iroquois; kidnaps Chief Donnacona

1541
- Meets stiff resistance from now wary Stadacona First Nation
- Returns home with "gold" and "diamonds" (iron pyrite and quartz)

JOHN CABOT
(a.k.a. Giovanni Caboto, Johan Cabot Montecalunyal, Antonio Gaboto)
Explored Canada:
1497

Nationality:
Italian (but working for the English)

JOHN CABOT
Stats:
- Claimed "New Founde Land" for King of England
- Grand Banks so teeming with cod they impeded progress of ships

Fate:
- Disappeared in 1498 on expedition in search of passage to the Orient

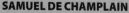

SAMUEL DE CHAMPLAIN
(a.k.a. The Father of New France)
Explored Canada:
1604–33

Nationality:
French

SAMUEL DE CHAMPLAIN

Stats:

1608
- Founds Québec City on site of former Stadacona First Nation settlement

1609
- Allies with Montagnais and Etchemin First Nations against the Iroquois

- Iroquois are wary of the French for the next 100 years

1613–14
- Explores as far as Lake Nipissing and Lake Huron

1629
- Surrenders Québec to the English

1633
- Returns to govern Québec after England cedes it back to France

WHAT'S REAL

All of the facts described on the card for each explorer did happen. Also, despite my best research, I cannot be certain that there was not actually a collection of "Explorers of Canada Trading Cards."

FIVE

Henry Hudson

Set adrift by his mutinous crew in 1611, Henry Hudson's fate remains a mystery. Now known more as a name than a man, he remains something of an enigma. Both the body of water, Hudson Bay, and therefore the eponymous, apostrophized "Hudson's Bay Company," are named after him.

Top Ten Reasons
It Sucks To Be Henry Hudson

10. Difficult to get fake ID made for getting into clubs since "????–1611" doesn't look very convincing on a birth certificate.

9. Sympathetic cartographers may have named a big bay and an impressive river after you, but your crew mutinied and set you adrift in a lifeboat in the Arctic—then you died (which never looks good on a résumé).

8. Your fellow countrymen revile you because you are an Englishman working for the Dutch. The Dutch?! What were you thinking? It's a wonder they didn't call you Benedict Arnold Hudson.

7. No one knows what you really looked like; conse-quently, you will forever be drawn with a big beard that makes you resemble a cross between Santa Claus and Grizzly Adams. This reduces your chances of scoring a date with famous miss-ing women from history, such as Amelia Earhart.

6. When they were handing out navigation skills, you took a double helping, leaving no room for leadership skills. This led to the mutiny and your subsequent death, thus severely lim-iting your availability in the job market.

5. Aside from popping up in interminable and quickly forgotten educational films, your only significant pop-culture appearance is as a ghost in *Rip Van Winkle*.

4. When you were stranded for the winter and your crew was starving, the book, *99 Meals to Make with Moss* had not yet been written.

3. When your crew told you they wanted to go back to England, you could have said "yes," but you didn't.

2. You'd already been dead for 59 years when the Hudson's Bay Company was incorporated—one of those scratchy, striped blankets sure would have come in handy in the lifeboat.

1. You died horribly while exploring a rugged new land, and now the department store that bears your name is a purveyor of the fragrance, "Celine Dion—Sensational"!

WHAT'S REAL

All true except for items that are obviously impossible owing to metaphysics or temporal anachronism. The date of Hudson's birth is unknown; he did work for the Dutch; he was cast adrift by his crew who had made repeated demands to return to England; and as far as I know, the book 99 Meals to Make with Moss *exists only in my head.*

SIX

Les Filles du Roi

In 1665, Jean Talon became the first intendant of New France and immediately set about building his back-woods colony into a holding France could be a bit more proud of. After he commissioned the colony's first census, Talon discovered three things: 1) the population was approximately 3200; 2) of those people, 720 were unmarried men; 3) there were only 45 unmarried women, some of whom were poor young women sent from France under the auspices of the King of France. Being a man of action, Talon asked the King to continue to pay for send poor young women across the Atlantic in order to marry hardy New France settlers. Between 1665 and 1673, nearly 800 "King's Daughters" (filles du roi) came to New France. If lurid, bodice-ripper novels had been written back then, one of them might have started like this.

La Coeur d'Une Fille du Roi
(The Heart of a King's Daughter)

CHAPTER 1

(Our heroine frets over her appearance, tries to keep from imagining a life she dares not hope for and demonstrates anachronistic awareness of the game of lacrosse, the accoutrements of which are shown on the next page.)

Lacrosse racquet and ball

1671

Madeleine Therriault stood serenely on the deck of the majestic ship as it coursed merrily through the seas…all right, she wasn't standing serenely so much as hanging her head over the side and vomiting copiously, but she was at least on her feet. And, truth be known, the ship wasn't really all that majestic—it was quite a common ship, but it had borne her and all the other *filles du roi* across the Atlantic without sinking, and for that alone it deserved some credit. And it wasn't exactly coursing merrily through the seas so much as it was limping into the harbour at Montréal after a difficult ocean crossing from France.

Breathing in the bracing salt air, the slender, attractive widow absently fingered the gold cross that hung tantalizingly in the cleft of her ravishing bosom…very well—her bosom was not so very ravishing, her figure not particularly slender, the cross was silver and the salty air made her feel rather ill.

Also, she was not a widow but an unmarried orphan. But—*mon dieu*—one had to look on the bright side. Madeleine had always been imaginative, and now she was trying to imagine what had ever possessed her to volunteer to make this voyage—ah, yes, poverty, that was it, as well as 50 livres, free transit across the ocean and the promise of a new life.

But what kind of life would that be? One of adventure and romance? Or one of tedium and drudgery? She had heard that some *filles du roi* were immediately married off to eager soldiers of a certain regiment—the Carignan-Salières Regiment—rough and ready men (probably dashingly unshaven as well) who were brought to New France to construct log forts (presumably with their excitingly calloused hands). Then they were charged with extermination of the Iroquois tribe but had failed to find any Iroquois, and many of the soldiers died during the winter—poor souls. As a reward for their hardships, the King gave several of them large seigneuries—long, manly plots of farmland that stretched (or did they thrust?) toward the river's moist edge in a most virile fashion.

Madeleine abruptly shook her statuesque head—it wouldn't do to get carried away; she could just as easily wind up married to a fishmonger. And, in truth, her head wasn't all that statuesque—in fact, there was a sizeable wart on the end of her nose, but it was a wart that used to fetch admiring looks from the street sweepers back in Paris. That was another thing that worried her—she was from Paris—what use could she possibly be in helping run a farm? She knew nothing about tending to crops or cattle. She didn't even know any folk remedies for getting rid of warts, though she suspected that they probably involved vinegar and, for some reason, dead cats.

They would soon be in sight of the pier, and most of the other *filles du roi* were coming up on deck now too. Madeleine eyed them appraisingly. There was Thérèse la Soeur, who really was a young attractive widow with a ravishing bosom. Madeleine could easily imagine that some handsome soldier with a large musket would snatch Thérèse up. Then there was Amelie Robespierre, a quick-witted country girl from Languedoc who had spent some time in a convent learning to read and write. Madeleine could see her marrying some powerful seigneur and even continuing to manage his affairs after he was horribly dismembered by wolves (she had heard of seigneurs' widows running their affairs, but the wolves were her own idea).

There was also Marie Priault. She was pretty enough in a sort of barn-yardy way. Madeleine imagined that Marie would marry a grenadier, perhaps one who had retired from soldiering and become a farmer. And perhaps their children would be good at that game, what was it called, lacrosse—the pastime of the Hurons she had heard, but much admired by many Frenchmen as well. Everyone else's future seemed so bright except hers. Would she be one of the few who did not marry? Who lost heart and returned to France, destined to become an old knitter woman, sitting grimly by and clacking her needles? What man would want a wart-nosed city girl with wide hips, wide everything else and an unravishing bosom?

But then the ship hove round the mouth of the bay and the pier came into sight. It was jammed with people shouting and waving at the ship. It was packed with...men! As the ship drew closer, Madeleine could see that the pier was jostling with tall men, short men, fat men and skinny men. There were men in the garb of soldiers, men who looked like they had been dismembered by wolves and men who reminded her of the wart-admiring street sweepers in Paris. She also noticed a few women standing by, but most of them were preoccupied with the bundles in their arms. But the men! They hooted. They hollered. They waved their hands and stomped their feet.

And Madeleine Therriault, the poor orphan from Paris, the stout young woman with a wart on the end of her nose, felt her heart rise into her throat. This was her new home, calling out with a thousand clamouring voices, shouting for her to get off the boat and start living already. It was the rest of her life waiting impatiently with arms thrown wide. It was the storybook she had always imagined, eagerly opening up in front of her.

WHAT'S REAL

Madeleine Therriault, Thérèse la Soeur and Amelie Robespierre are all fictional characters, but Marie Priault was a real fille du roi *who married a grenadier turned farmer named Pierre Joffrion who had been with the Carignan-Salières Regiment. According to family lore, Hockey Hall of Famer Bernie Geoffrion is descended directly from Marie and Pierre, hence all the lacrosse innuendo in the piece above.*

Although not referred to in this story, one sometimes encounters the idea that many of the filles du roi *were prostitutes—this is complete nonsense; many were girls from poor families, sometimes rural, sometimes from the city. Some were educated in convents and were quite literate. The occasional destitute widow also chose to come to the New World in search of a better life. Eager men would come down to the docks to wait for the next shipment of women. Widows of seigneurs were known to run farms after the demise of their husbands, but the supposed remedy for warts involving "vinegar" and "dead cats" I freely admit to having made up wholesale.*

SEVEN

New France Plays
its Cards Right

Nowadays, our neighbours south of the border frequently observe that Canadians have "funny money" (largely because our paper money comes in more colours than just "Conformity Green"). But what would Americans have thought of the money that circulated in New France during the late 17th and early 18th centuries?

Au poisson! (Go Fish!): These playing cards would have been worth a fortune in New France, but unless you have a time machine *and* a seriously indifferent monarch, don't get any big ideas.

August 6, 1691—New France

Cher Maman,

   You will be glad to know that
my ship arrived safely here in New
France two days ago. I know you still
believe my intent to set up shop here
as a scribe to read and write documents for the illiterate (of whom there
are many) is a futile venture. In vain
did I argue that such a career was the
only one I might be suited for after
a lifetime spent forbidden, by you,
from playing outside with other children. Instead, your idea of play was
to make me sit inside for hours to
practise my penmanship; for "fun,"
I was "allowed" to copy the handwriting
of others.
   And still you express wonder that
I should want to venture to the New
World in order to drink deeply of those
fresh airs whose healthful inhalation
you have, until now, so diligently
denied me.
   You shall no doubt be pleased to
know that I most likely will not
need to enter into my intended employment as a "screever" (or so I am told

the English call them) because all
of the fantastical rumours we have
heard at home are true: here in New
France, *playing cards* are accepted as
money! I can still remember your horror
that I should want to bring something
so *bourgeois* as a pack of playing cards
on a sea voyage of at least 12 weeks.
But I held my ground, correctly assuming that there would be many long hours
of uncomfortable and perilous leisure
during which this sort of distraction
might be welcome.

Furthermore, contrary to your asser-
tions otherwise, the rolling seas are
not a stable enough medium in which to
keep up my penmanship drills; the heav-
ing ocean is an entirely inappropriate
environment for such an undertaking.

At any rate, here I am in New France
with a deck of playing cards worth a
fortune! Of course, it is not quite so
simple as that. People tell me that the
government here has been doing this sort
of thing since 1685. The Intendant
of Justice, Police and Finance at the
time—one Jacques Demeulle—found himself
in a predicament of not inconsiderable
perplexity; there was no new coinage
arriving from France, and Demeulle had

not only to pay his soldiers but also had to find some way to keep commerce flowing in the colony. So being a wealthy man, Demeulle wrote promissory notes—worth, say, 50 *livres*—on the backs of playing cards, cut them into quarters and distributed them to soldiers. The soldiers then used them as payment when purchasing goods from the inhabitants at large. And then a few months later, on a set day, the local merchants could get their playing card money redeemed by Demeulle from his own coffers.

It saved the Intendant all sorts of bother because he did not have to constantly hand out money from his strong box, but instead could do it all at once on a set day.

This so-called card money quickly caught on, and it circulates more or less at face value, being, for all intents and purposes, as good as the real thing.

Imagine that! An official government issuing money made out of paper! These promissory notes written on bits of worthless wood pulp are the sort of thing one expects between friends, but from His Majesty's Government one expects good solid specie of gold or silver.

Of course, *cher maman,* as you and I know, the government at home strongly disapproves—as I recall, they worry that such notes are easy to forge since their only endorsement is the spidery handwriting of a government official on the reverse side. And it is in that spidery handwriting, *cher maman,* that my future fortune lies. You will be pleased to learn that the current Intendant's handwriting bears more than a passing resemblance to that of your brother, *mon oncle Antoine,* whose handwriting you used to encourage me to emulate as I sat at the window and watched the other children play *petanque* on the lawns.

I have already masterfully copied the Intendant's signature onto at least half the deck I have brought with me and should have enough money to spend the winter in a state of luxurious excess.

The *non*-sayers over there at home may complain that these practices devalue and debase French currency, but I say it saves the King a lot of trouble as he does not have to worry about shipping large amounts of gold and silver overseas where they may be captured by the English.

Besides, the feeling here is that the King cannot be bothered to actually send real money over (or at least repeatedly fails to do so), and that is why we have playing card money to begin with.

And there you have it, *cher maman*— once I have redeemed my cards for real silver and gold, I will send some of it home to you.

Your loving Louis

WHAT'S REAL

Playing card money was used (on and off) in New France from 1685 to the early 1750s. By the last few decades though, the playing cards were replaced by treasury notes, made with a real printing press on card stock in order to make them more difficult to forge. But even then, counterfeiting was a problem, and one Louis Mallet, along with his wife, Marie Moore, were hanged on September 2, 1736, for the crime of forging card money.

There were pros and cons of card money; on the one hand it helped the beleaguered French treasury to carry on operations in the New World, but on the other hand, it triggered some degree of inflation and, in the end, was simply a band-aid solution to an economy plagued by a chronic shortage of funds.

While governments had long issued paper bonds and documents that could be redeemed by other governments or stakeholders, the use of card money in New France is often cited as the earliest intro-duction of government-backed paper currency (money that could be used by regular citizens in day-to-day transactions) to North America. Funny money indeed!

EIGHT

The Fight for the Fur Trade

For almost 200 years, North America was the battleground for an epic struggle between rival interests. Their goal? To gain the upper hand in the fur trade, a difficult but highly profitable enterprise that involved transporting fur pelts (mainly beaver) over hazardous routes (mainly riverways) and on to Europe where the pelts were made into garments (mainly hats) for the wealthy. The problem was that (mainly English) kings and governments were fond of granting monopolies to certain groups (mainly the Hudson's Bay Company). In theory, a "monopoly" meant no one except the HBC was legally allowed to trap beaver. But how do you enforce a monopoly on thousands of square miles of land that is (mainly) uninhabited?

Fur-Trade Monopoly
A Suspiciously Familiar Board Game

HOW TO PLAY

Who are the players?

THE HUDSON'S BAY COMPANY (a British firm) is trying to enforce its royally chartered monopoly to trade furs in the vast lands that drain into Hudson Bay.

IROQUOIS FIRST NATIONS allied with the HBC or other British interests.

The HBC's opponents are principally:

- FRENCH FUR TRADERS who themselves enjoyed a monopoly throughout most of the 1600s until British interests started moving in

- FIRST NATIONS GROUPS allied with the French

- THE NORTH WEST COMPANY (NWC) and other rival British interests

How long should a game last?

About 150 years. If you can somehow manage to be playing between the years 1670 and 1820, this will lend an air of authenticity to the proceedings.

Are players expected to actually respect the HBC's monopoly?

Well, no—where would the fun be in that?

RULES OF THE GAME

1. Each player will choose one (1) of the following six gaming pieces:

2. Please note that we have observed the following:

- Players who choose the Beaver tend to lose almost immediately.

- Those who choose the Beaver Skin Hat enjoy what may at first seem like unlimited success, but the hat finally proves to be a passing fad.

- Players who choose the Birchbark Canoe will wind up doing most of the work upon which the success of other players is built.

- Players who choose the HBC Charter will ultimately prevail no matter how unimaginatively they play the game.

- Those who choose the Fleur-de-Lys will ultimately be vanquished but will never, ever, ever, ever be able to accept this fact.

- And to those players choosing the Tomahawk: your struggle continues.

NOTE: Players wishing to construct their own playing pieces may make the following substitutions: for the Beaver, use a Nickel; for the Beaver Skin Hat, use a morsel of beaver tail pastry (messy, yes, but undeniably delicious); for the Birchbark Canoe, use any spare fortune cookies that may be lying around—their squashy shape more or less corresponds to the battered physique of a birchbark canoe that has been on a long voyage; for the HBC Charter, use any piece of HBC paraphernalia you may have: price tags, Bay bucks and so forth; for the Fleur-de-Lys, substitute anything that, for you, represents Québec (for example, bottlecaps from *Maudite* beer, keychains with the *Canadiens* logo, what have you); and finally, for the Tomahawk, use anything that, for you, represents a broken promise (for example, IOUs from the tooth fairy, promissory notes for ponies; ticket stubs from the second *X-Files* movie, and so forth.

3. The player holding the HBC Charter game piece will always be given the first roll of the dice,

an opportunity they will likely squander or execute poorly.

4. Players will move their gaming pieces ahead as many spaces as are determined by the roll of the dice and their proficiency at befriending First Nations peoples.

5. When a player lands on a plot of unoccupied land, he or she may purchase said plot in exchange for precious beaver belts, addictive rum or vast quantities of spilt blood.

6. Players may build forts on plots of land owned by them (or any other player for that matter), provided they have beaver pelts, rum and enough blood for shedding.

7. If a player should land on a plot of land occupied by any other player, both sides should expect a decrease in profit and an increase in bloodshed.

8. The holder of the HBC Charter will stick to the shores of Hudson Bay, and for the first few decades, at least, will not even try to enforce the monopoly inland, thereby giving the other players a chance to move in.

9. If a player should land on either of the squares marked "Good for HBC" or "Bad for HBC," the said player will take a card from the top of the appropriate pile and follow the instructions thereon. Those cards are as follows:

Good for HBC

1670

HBC is incorporated and King Charles of England grants HBC a monopoly on trading furs in all the lands that drain into Hudson Bay.

☞ Collect 1000 beaver pelts, or pay 1000 pelts, depending on your affiliation.

Bad for HBC

1686

The French Compagnie du Nord conducts a daring raid to win control of the HBC's forts in the James Bay area.

☞ Move ahead three spaces or back three spaces depending on your affiliation.

Good for HBC

1689

After the French send 40 envoys of the Onandaga First Nation back to France as slaves, the Iroquois lead retaliatory attacks, starting with the Lachine Massacre and setting off a decade of First Nations attacks in New France.

☞ Either sit tight or move back three spaces depending on your affiliation.

Bad for HBC

1697

Despite being outnumbered 3-to-1, French daredevil Pierre d'Iberville defeats English forces in a pitched sea battle to take control of HBC's York Factory on the shores of Hudson Bay. It stays in French hands for the next 16 years.

☞ *Collect or sacrifice 16 years worth of beaver pelts depending on your affiliation.*

Bad for HBC

1701

A peace treaty between New France and the Iroquois puts an end to years of conflict. The French can now focus solely on their conflict with the British interests.

☞ *Build five forts or tear down five forts based on your affiliation.*

Good for HBC

1713

After spending 11 years fighting Queen Anne's war, which finally ends with the Treaty of Utrecht, France pays for its losses in Europe by relinquishing its claims on both the St. Lawrence heartland and the maritime region of Acadia.

☞ *Sit back and relax or retreat in shame depending on your affiliation.*

Good for HBC

1763

After decades of competition and conflict, the Seven Years' War puts an end to French dominance in the New World. The HBC's influence predominates, and experienced French *coureur de bois* start to freelance for their former rival.

☞ *Expand or reduce your sphere of influence depending on your affiliation.*

Bad for HBC

1779

Disgruntled fur traders in Montréal form the NWC. It attracts experienced employees of both British and French extraction. The NWC ambitiously pushes into the interior, giving the HBC a run for their money.

☞ *Expand or reduce your sphere of influence depending on your affiliation.*

Good for HBC

1791

In spite of appeals from the now powerful NWC, British Prime Minister William Pitt refuses to revoke the HBC's monopoly.

☞ *Either sit tight or move back three spaces depending on your affiliation.*

Bad for HBC

1793

On July 22, NWC explorer Alexander Mackenzie becomes the
first European to reach the Pacific Ocean by cutting across
the northern half of the American continent. Completely useless
from a practical point of view, his accomplishment has huge
symbolic significance.

— ∽ —

☞ *Celebrate or complacently do nothing according to your affiliation.*

Good for HBC

1800

Now a disgruntled trader himself, Alexander Mackenzie joins
the upstart XY Company, which is a blow to the NWC and so
good for the HBC.

— ∽ —

☞ *Stand united or fall divided according to your affiliation.*

Bad for HBC

1804

The XY company merges back into the NWC, and HBC's
opponents are united once more.

— ∽ —

☞ *Bite nails anxiously or proceed with confidence depending on
your affiliation.*

Good for HBC

1821

Despite owing more than £100,000 to British stakeholders, the HBC manages to gain the upper hand, and what should have been a merger becomes a takeover; the HBC now owns the NWC and has achieved total dominance.

☞ *Hoot and holler and wave your donut.*

Bad for HBC

1821–present

In the following years, the Bay becomes a purveyor of scratchy blankets, electric eggbeaters and any number of questionable celebrity fragrances. Stamina, fortitude and ambition are supplanted by bureaucratic governance. Once you were an empire; now you are a department store.

☞ *Cry into your beer.*

MILD WINTER	YORK FACTORY 500 pelts	GOOD FOR HBC	FORT DAUPHIN 100 pelts	FORT EDMONTON 300 pelts	FORT CARLTON 500 pelts	GET BESIEGED
FORT DOUGLAS 200 pelts						FORT FRONTENAC 500 pelts
BAD FOR HBC			Good for HBC place cards here			GOOD FOR HBC
FORT WILLIAM 100 pelts		MONOPOLIZE The Fur Trade				FORT McMURRAY 100 pelts
FORT GIBRALTAR 500 pelts						BAD FOR HBC
FORT ROUGE 300 pelts		Bad for HBC place cards here				MOOSE FACTORY 100 pelts
LONG PORTAGE	FORT PASKOYA 300 pelts	BAD FOR HBC	KOOTENAE HOUSE 500 pelts	FORT BOURBON 300 pelts	GOOD FOR HBC	ALLEZ! Collect 200 pelts

NINE

The Acadian Expulsion

Canada's French and British overlords spilled a lot of blood to compete for the resource-rich North American colony. On both sides, though, were farmers, merchants and families—regular people—who just wanted to get on with their lives. On the French side, vibrant agricultural communities had taken root in present-day Nova Scotia and New Brunswick, then called Acadia. By the time the French ceded Acadia to the English in 1713, the Acadians were already a distinct society and didn't particularly care who claimed to be governing them. Successive British governments let them do as they pleased as long as they did not side with the French (which they were happy not to do anyway). But by the mid-1700s, the fight for control of Canada was reaching its peak, and the Acadians were about to get caught in the middle. Some of them might have benefitted from having, at the very least, a travel brochure or something.

CONQUEST TRAVEL

presents

Expulsion Vacations *

*An exclusive service for French settlers in Acadia, courtesy of the British Crown

☞

The following *deluxe* displacement packages are available for the years 1755–62.

Why YOU DESERVE our special offer...

- You have worked hard for 40 years hewing wood and tilling soil to develop a thriving agrarian society.

- We Limeys are worried that in our next war with France you will choose a side, and it won't be ours (although you've had plenty of chances to do this but haven't).

- You refuse to swear an oath of loyalty to the English but appease us, your British overlords, by swearing not one, not two, but three different oaths of neutrality.

- You live peaceably but refuse to pay your taxes.

- We are English. You are French. Nuff said.

To prepare for YOUR VOYAGE, we hereby...

- Forbid you from building or importing boats so that you could willingly move to other French colonies (because all

you Frenchies might gang up on us
Pommey Bastards if we let too many
of you live together).

- Forbid you from selling any of your
property or livestock so that you
might be able to accrue any sort
of wealth or assets.

EXCITING OVERSEAS DESTINATIONS

*include...***England! France!**

As well as many quaint ports of call up and
down the eastern seaboard,

in addition to...
Scenic Landlocked Locales!

**Connecticut • New York • Maryland
Pennsylvania • North Carolina • Georgia
Massachusetts • Main • New Brunswick
Prince Edward Island • Nova Scotia
Québec • Louisiana**

To expedite your voyage, Commanding
Officer Sir Charles Lawrence has given *special
orders:*

*" I would have you not wait for the Wives
and Children...but Ship Off the Men without them."*

and

"...you must proceed by the most vigorous measures possible...in depriving those who shall escape of all means of shelter or support by burning their houses and destroying everything that may afford them the means of subsistence..."

OUR SHIPS are the most miserable transport money can buy! If they don't sink and carry you to a watery grave, they also make excellent breeding grounds for such favourite maladies as Small Pox, the Typhoid *and* Yellow Fever. And in the unlikely event that your life in Acadia has been a lonely one, NEVER FEAR—by maximizing our capacity, we can pack you in so tightly that you likely won't be able to breathe!

PACKAGES AND DEPARTURE DATES

- Sept. 5, 1755: Kiss your wife and family goodbye, because this is the day it all gets underway! First you'll gather at the picturesque local church to hear a proclamation that designates you as "non-citizens." Then you'll discover that your farms and all of your property

☞

are going to be destroyed. Best of all, more than 2000 of you will be herded directly onto ships—your family will never know what happened to you (presuming they even survive our vicious and destructive attacks on your former homesteads). Expect about 5000 more of your compatriots to follow in the ensuing years.

- 1758: Just when you thought the mid-century blahs were here to stay (getting back on your feet and rebuilding your communities is just *so* tedious), here we come again to kick your Froggy Asses from here to the ends of the earth. This time, some of you may be lucky enough to go to special camps in Britain where you'll spend years and years and years. By the time we finish up in 1762, you can expect that out of the 23,000 of you, only about 10,000 will survive.

PRICE

Your dignity, your possessions, your property, your families, your homes, years of hard work—your lives.

WHAT'S REAL

Everything mentioned actually happened (except for the printing of this patently ridiculous travel brochure). What's more amazing is what happened afterwards—many Acadians came back! Some returned from England, France and elsewhere in North America only to discover that their homes had been destroyed or given to British settlers (in some cases to highland Scots who had just been displaced from their own homes in Scotland). Some elected to stay, but this time they took the oath of loyalty that the British demanded. Others dispersed into different parts of North America, including Québec and New Orleans (where they became known as "Cajuns").

In December 2003, the Canadian government acknowledged that the "Great Upheaval" (Le Grande Dérangement) had been wrong—but stopped short of actually apologizing. It was kind of a moot point anyway—all the displaced Acadians had been dead for 200 years.

TEN

The Battle of the Plains of Abraham

September 13, 2009, was the 250th anniversary of the Battle of the Plains of Abraham, now widely considered to have been the death stroke for French rule in Canada. For the anniversary there had been plans to stage a re-enactment, but there were storms of protest and threats of civil disobedience from Québecers tired of being reminded that their province is still a part of Canada. And so the re-enactment was called off, but what might have happened if it had taken place?

A Re-enactment

RON: Hello to everyone here and all the viewers at home. Welcome to the 250th anniversary re-enactment of the Battle of the Plains of Abraham.

DON: There's nobody here, Ron, and there's nobody watching at home.

RON: Well, I'm sure that somebody's watching—

DON: No, Ron, nobody's watching, and do you know why nobody's watching? Because the stupid producers decided to stage this thing in real time. It's two o'clock in the morning right now and the

British are still anchored upstream just getting ready to cast off. People get up at two o'clock in the morning to watch the Olympics, Ron, not to watch a bunch of Little Lord Fauntleroys run around in pretty jackets and shoot blanks at each other. There's *nothing* going on, and even if there was, it's pitch black and we can't see anything.

RON: Well, how about that gunfire I can hear? That's something.

DON: Yeah, it's a diversionary bombardment that the British are staging farther upriver, and they've been doing it *all night* and it's starting to drive me crazy. How am I supposed to get any sleep?

RON: Ah, but that diversionary bombardment worked, didn't it, Don? It made the French general, Montcalm, believe that the attack would come elsewhere.

DON: Ron, the British could have farted into the wind and the French would have thought the attack was going to be somewhere else, because the idea of attacking a location where you have to get your troops to climb up 150 feet of steep cliff-side in the pitch dark is completely insane.

RON: But that's just what General Wolfe did.

DON: Sadly, it's the very reason we're here right now—at two o'clock in the morning.

RON: Five after two now actually. Don, since we've got a bit of time until they drop the puck—I mean, until they start the fight—maybe you could give us some background.

DON: Aw, whatever—it's the Seven Years' War—blah blah blah—the French have been kicking English ass pretty good, but you know how I feel about the French, Ron.

RON: I sure do, Don. Now, as I understand it, General Wolfe's forces have recently been trounced in their attack on Montmorency.

DON: If this was a seven-game series, the French would be leading three to two.

RON: Tell us a bit about the players.

DON: Well, of course, the two enforcers are Montcalm for the French, and Wolfe for the British.

RON: Let's start with Montcalm.

DON: Well, he's French, Ron, and you know how I feel about the French.

RON: I sure do, Don.

DON: Actually, Montcalm is an OK general, but he just doesn't seal the deal.

RON: You're referring to his habit of fighting the British off but not actually going after them even when he has them on the run?

DON: Yeah, it's like he can get the puck out of his end zone, but he just doesn't take any shots on the other team's net.

RON: Montcalm is on record as saying that he could defend this location with 100 men and that the British would need wings to get up the cliffs.

DON: Yup—he's released most of his local militia to go help with the harvest, and he doesn't seem to realize that if you have ground to walk on, even if it's very steep ground, you don't need wings provided you have legs. Now, call it 20/20 hindsight, Ron, but it's pretty obvious to me that the British troops have legs. It's actually a pre-requisite for being a soldier.

RON: And what about Wolfe?

DON: Oh, geez. Where am I supposed to start with this guy?

RON: Wolfe hasn't been at the top of his game has he?

DON: No, he's been sick. Actually, Wolfe has been sick his whole life, but earlier this month he had a wicked fever from kidney stones, and his doctor bled him and gave him a bunch of drugs.

RON: So Wolfe is weakened and possibly muddled from medication?

DON: Ron, some people like to think that Wolfe is stoned out of his gourd on powerful opiates, but I think—like you say—he's just feverish and, as you know, this kid is driven to succeed. I mean, he's only 32 and he's a general. Montcalm is 47. That takes some kind of moxie.

RON: Do you think there's any truth to the rumour that Wolfe plays for the pink team and not the blue team?

DON: What do you mean? The French uniforms are blue, but the English uniforms are red, not pink—oh! I see what you're getting at.

RON: He's kind of effeminate. He's not that interested in girls...

DON: Truthfully, Ron, I think he's just focused 110 percent on his career.

(Commercial Break)

RON: Welcome back to the 250th anniversary re-enactment of the Battle of the Plains of Abraham. It's the top of the hour—over to you, Don...Don?... Don, wake up!

DON: Uhhh...are the Timbits here yet?

RON: No, the Timbits are not here, but it's the top of the hour, and we need some sort of commentary from you.

DON: Top of the hour? It's 3:00 AM!

RON: That's right—it's the top of the hour, so let me just turn out the lights in the booth here and maybe we can see something out there.

DON: The production assistant was supposed to bring me Timbits.

RON: OK, the lights are out now, so let's see what we can see by the moonlight. It looks to me like there's some sort of movement out there on the river, is that right, Don?

DON: Well, duh—that's the English ships and boats sailing down river and being stopped by the French.

RON: Being stopped by the French? Shouldn't that scuttle the whole attack?

DON: It should, but it doesn't, because even though this is an ill-considered enterprise, the English have horseshoes dripping out of their asses.

RON: You mean they're lucky?

DON: Lucky doesn't even start to describe it. First off, there've been boatloads of French soldiers going up and down the river all night, and so the sentries on shore figure it's just one of them.

RON: OK.

DON: So what's happening now is that the sentry on shore is calling out in French to challenge them. The British have actually come slightly prepared, because in the lead boat they've put an officer named Simon Fraser, who can speak French. When the French sentry on shore calls out "Who's there?" Fraser replies, in French, "France! Long live the King!" And the sentry asks which regiment they're with, and Fraser says they're part of the *De la Reine* regiment. What Fraser doesn't know is that the *De la Reine* regiment is now under a different command and is off doing other things. But—and this is a big but—the French sentry on shore doesn't seem to know this either, so he asks them why they didn't just speak up at the beginning, and Fraser says they're worried about being overheard by the British, and so the sentry lets them go—this is all happening in pitch blackness remember, because it's 3:00 AM. It's 3:00 AM, and I still don't have my Timbits!

(Commercial Break)

RON: Alright, I can see the first faint flush of dawn creeping over the horizon, so let's do this thing shall we, Don?

DON: OK, I've had some coffee, I've had my Timbits and I'm ready to go!

RON: Now, who's that lone figure running through the trees there?

DON: Oh, well, that's easy—the English have landed now, they've reached the top of the cliff, and there's been a minor skirmish with the French, so it's a French messenger going to warn Montcalm that the attack is underway.

RON: Wait a minute! The French get a warning and they don't even do anything?

DON: It's not Montcalm's fault though—as you can see, the messenger's arrived at the camp and he's talking to one of Montcalm's officers there and—

RON: And the officer is sending him away, and it looks like—

DON: The officer's going back to bed, Ron—he doesn't want to wake Montcalm because he's decided that the messenger is completely insane.

RON: Well, for goodness' sake! A thing like that!

DON: You have to remember that the British have had Québec City under siege for months. And because the defence of the city itself is so solid, all Wolfe can do from an offensive standpoint is run around the countryside and make life miserable for the locals. Over the summer his forces have destroyed more than 1400 French farms and homesteads—Wolfe is deep into the other team's end zone, but he just can't get into the crease, and he's being a real prick about it.

RON: And I know how you feel about the French, Don.

DON: So everybody's sort of expecting him to do something a bit crazy, but nothing *this* crazy.

RON: It's getting lighter now, and you can see the British troops coming over the top of the cliff there. Wow, they're making really good time and coming up quickly. I can't believe there isn't any opposition at this point.

DON: Wolfe will never know how lucky he is because normally there's at least one sentry on patrol in this neck of the woods, but last night one of the sentry's horses was stolen, and his two back-up horses both went lame.

(Commercial Break)

RON: Well, it's between 6:30 and 7:00 AM now, and it looks like the battle is nearly here. Don, tell us what we're seeing here.

DON: You're seeing pretty much what Montcalm is seeing, and that's a line of British redcoats— seven brigades—stretching for half a mile across the Plains of Abraham.

RON: Normally the redcoats would be three deep, wouldn't they?

DON: That's right, Ron, but Wolfe has them only two deep today because he has to cover a lot of ground.

RON: Numerically, these armies are a pretty even match, each with about 4500 men—some put it as low as 3500 each—but that's about what we're looking at, give or take.

DON: The numbers may be close, but these are two different armies, Ron. Wolfe probably has slightly fewer men, but they're all regular troops, and that means they're professionals—disciplined and tough—always waiting for the next order and not getting distracted by what's happening around them.

RON: But Montcalm has an uneven mixture of regulars and part-time militia made up of farmers and other locals.

DON: Yeah, he's coaching a farm-league team, but the opposition has all professional players, and Wolfe is on record as saying he would rather die than lose Québec, and, as it turns, that's exactly what happens.

RON: Y'know, the major drawback for Montcalm here is that he's used to fighting big set-piece battles with his troops in tight, disciplined formations, but he just doesn't have a team—sorry, an army—with enough training and discipline to pull it off.

DON: No, he doesn't. Now, if you take a look out there, you can see that Montcalm has mustered some Indians—sorry, some Aboriginals—sorry, some members of the First Nations—to play interference— I mean, to act as snipers—off to the side in those woods, and so the British are taking some fire.

RON: They may be taking fire, but they're not really flinching. They're not moving at all; they're just standing there. That's gotta be unnerving for Montcalm.

DON: The British will probably clean those snipers out before the morning's over anyway, but now you can see that Wolfe is ordering all his men to lie down to avoid being hit.

RON: And if I recall correctly, Montcalm thinks they're entrenching and decides he should attack soon.

(Commercial Break)

RON: It's just before 10:00 AM now, and you can see that Montcalm is starting to order his men into formations.

DON: And sure enough, Ron, you can see that he's trying to organize them into columns so they can march forward and punch through the British lines like a fork through a steak, but I don't think they have the discipline.

RON: The sad thing is that this is where Montcalm really blows it. Normally he's very patient, methodical and cautious, but now he decides to rush in and attack.

DON: You're right, Ron. All he has to do is wait for reinforcements to arrive from behind the British, and the redcoats would be trapped. Then Montcalm could attack and force the British back down the cliff, and the French reinforcements could pick them off from the landing site.

RON: But we both know that's not going to happen.

DON: Nope.

RON: And there it is—the French have started the advance.

DON: You know, another problem for Montcalm is that the militia half of his army has civilian rifles with greater firing ranges than the military muskets that the regulars have.

RON: But he doesn't order anyone to start firing until they're within musket range.

DON: And Montcalm doesn't know it yet, but Wolfe his given has own soldiers strict orders not to open fire until the enemy is just 40 yards away.

RON: Ouch!

DON: And there it is—the French militia have broken ranks already, and they're not really advancing so much as stuttering forward and firing at will. The regulars and the militia are completely failing to work together. I've seen schoolyard games of Red Rover played with more discipline, Ron.

RON: That big set-piece battle that Montcalm was hoping for isn't going to happen.

DON: Nope, his troops are playing two different games—they're not playing as a team.

RON: Ohhh! Wolfe takes a shot in the wrist.

DON: Yes, his wrist is looking pretty limp there, and...he's bound it up with a handkerchief it looks like.

RON: Here we go! The French are bearing down on the British now—they're about 60 yards away—but the British are starting to fire from either end of their line—and look at that! The French are dropping like flies.

DON: That's partly because Wolfe has ordered his men to load their muskets with two balls each, so the first volley is just murderous.

RON: The French won't like that.

DON: I think they already don't like it.

RON: OK, they're 40 yards away now, and pretty soon Wolfe should be giving the two regiments in the middle their firing orders and—

DON: There it is—

RON: Oh, it's a slaughter—those double musket balls have blown the middle out of the French line.

DON: It's really just a mopping-up process now, and you can see that one of the Highland regiments has actually slung their rifles and taken out their claymore broadswords to hack away at the retreating French.

RON: Wow, the actual battle hardly took any time at all.

DON: Some people think that once the firing began in earnest it could have been over in as little as 12 minutes.

RON: Well, it's certainly over now, Don. Both Wolfe and Montcalm are dying from their wounds of course, and that's about it, I think. Wait a minute?! What's that I can see through the smoke? There— coming over the cliff!

DON: Well, look at that—it's the protesters—an hour late and a dollar short. SORRY, BOYS, BUT THE BATTLE'S OVER AND DONE WITH! IT WAS OVER AND DONE WITH 250 YEARS AGO! Y'know, Ron, these guys just don't understand that what's done is done.

RON: Well, you could say that about the re-enactors, too.

DON: That's true, you could, but you know how I feel about the French.

RON: I sure do, Don.

WHAT'S REAL

Anything that Ron and Don say directly relating to the battle itself has been either researched or conjectured by the authors listed in the sources at the end of this book. There was indeed going to be a re-enactment on September 13, 2009, but it was cancelled after numerous objections. If, however, the re-enactment had taken place, it is highly doubtful it would have been staged in real time.

The things missing from this tongue-in-cheek look at the battle are the many complex factors that came into play, the large supporting cast of important players besides Wolfe and Montcalm and, finally, the battle's true place as one of many smaller conflicts fought in Europe and North America as part of the Seven Years' War.

ELEVEN

Peter Pond Discovers the Alberta Tar Sands

*When he wasn't busy being repeatedly tried for mur-
der, Peter Pond (1739–1807) did some exploring and,
among other things, noticed that local First Nations
people used some sticky black stuff that oozed out of
the ground to seal and patch their birchbark canoes.*

HERITAGE MCMOMENT #2

FROM: Richard Wanker
Broadcast Executive,
Historical TV Channel

TO: Mordant Wit
Freelance Writer

Hi again Mordant,

So glad that you're on board again
for Heritage McMoment #2: "Peter Pond
Discovers the Alberta Tar Sands." :)

☞

I know we've had our creative differences over the first Heritage McMoment about potlatches—that's my bad :(I guess I should have explained that what we're looking for is the spirit of Canadian history and not so much the facts. Once again, I've taken the liberty of typing up something along the lines of what we want.

I learned a lot of new things while doing this one—for instance, I didn't know that when they first saw oil oozing out of the sand, they called it "bitch-human"—did you know that? I wonder why they would have called it "bitch-human"—maybe it's some kind of Indian—sorry, Aboriginal—term. Would you mind looking into that? I don't think we need to include it in the McMoment—I'm just curious, and I assume that, as a writer, you have plenty of free time on your hands.

Once again, looking forward to your feedback,
Richard (Dick) Wanker

Heritage McMoment #2:
Peter Pond Discovers the Alberta Tar Sands

Suggestions for visuals: I figure that first we'd see Peter Pond. He should be very "explorery" looking, with a beard and all that—and he's watching the Indians—sorry, the Natives—patch their canoes with this oozing stuff that comes out of the sand, and we just take it from there.

NARRATOR	WRITER'S NOTES
In 1778, Peter Pond—an explorer for the North West Company—discovered the Alberta tar sands, though he didn't know it at the time.	
(Peter notices the Indians patching their canoes with black, sticky gorp.)	
PETER POND	
What is that you're patching your canoe with?	
INDIAN	*You insufferable ass! It's not "bitch-human," it's "bitumen"! I take it from this that you've only heard people say the word and never actually seen it in print. Please note that I use old-fashioned punctuation for*
My people call it "bitch-human." It seeps from the sands and bubbles to the surface of vast steaming pits.	

☞

emphasis and not moronic emoticons. >:(

"Bitumen" is NOT an Aboriginal word—it's an Old English word that means "resin" or "pitch." Only Europeans would have used that term.

PETER POND

You know what, my feather-headed friend? I have a feeling there might just be something in this.

(Peter winks at the camera.)

Besides objecting to the offensive term "feather-headed," I have to point out that Peter Pond didn't give a damn about the so-called bitumen fountains. He was looking for new fur-trade routes and nothing more. He didn't think there was any use for it other than for repairing canoes.

NARRATOR

Peter Pond—he killed three men, but we love him anyway, and even though he has nothing to do with today's oil industry, we celebrate him because he was the first white man to discover oil in Alberta, and really, who cares about Indians who actually discovered the oil and used it to patch their canoes? Not us.

Wow, I take everything back about you being an insufferable ass—this last part really tells it like it is, but do you think the broadcaster will let you get away with it? Irony isn't exactly their strong point.

FROM: Richard Wanker
Broadcast Executive,
Historical TV Channel

TO: Mordant Wit
Freelance Writer

Hi Mordant,

I'm really glad you liked the script, but I didn't really understand the last part about "irony"—everybody knows that Alberta's main export is oil and not iron. Anyway, I meant every word I wrote in that last part, but it's your name that's going on it anyhow… so—you're welcome!

I asked my assistant and he says "insufferable ass" is the latest street lingo for "super awesome"—so thanks—that really means a lot to me.

Looking forward to working on the next Heritage McMoment with you. It's going to be about Mary Ann Shadd. She was the first woman in Canada and the first black woman in North America to found, edit and publish a newspaper.

Sincerely,
Richard (Dick) Wanker

WHAT'S REAL

Peter Pond did notice First Nations peoples patching their canoes with bitumen and noted it as a curiosity, but otherwise showed little interest. And it was First Nations peoples who discovered the stuff—Peter Pond was just an observer.

TWELVE

Alexander Mackenzie's Voyage to the Pacific

On July 22, 1793, Alexander Mackenzie reached the Pacific Ocean after a long and arduous journey across North America. He was ostensibly looking for a quicker route to the Pacific Ocean to increase the North West Company's fur trade, but by the time he and his small party had arrived, it was obvious that the route was too difficult to be practical (profitable) for trading. Nonetheless, within his lifetime, Mackenzie was hailed as a hero, not least for completing a round trip of 2300 miles with a party of seven voyageurs, two First Nations guides and a dog—all in a birchbark canoe 25 feet long and loaded with 3000 pounds of supplies. However, it is plain from Mackenzie's journals that not all of his men were necessarily eager to continue. If one member of Mackenzie's company had kept a journal, this might have been it.

The Unwilling Voyageur
(excerpts from the Journal of Jacques Beauchamp)

JAN. 1, 1793—FORT FORK

IT IS THE FIRST DAY OF A NEW YEAR, and I have decided to start keeping a journal. I sit by the fire at night and watch Mackenzie scratching away in his notebook

First, imagine your job is to paddle 2300 kilometres in a canoe like this. Assume that you have to stop every day to repair it, and then imagine carrying the canoe for significant parts of the journey as well. Next, imagine that your heart isn't really into it in the first place, and you'll get a sense of what it must have been like to be a reluctant voyageur.

―⁕―

and I think to myself, "If Alexander Mackenzie can keep a journal, why should not Jacques Beauchamp keep also a journal?" I know how to write. I even know how to read. And so why not? Besides, if Monsieur Mackenzie is to lead us on a mad dash to the Atlantic Ocean, then Jacques Beauchamp *(c'est moi)* does not want his to be the only version of events.

Here is the story so far. I joined Mackenzie's crew back in Grand Portage. I heard he was looking for men and so I presented myself. He looked me up and down and said in his hard Scotch accent, "Och, aye, hoot mahn, well, if no one more fitting turns up then I suppose you shall have to do." And then, the seven of us (not including Mackenzie and the two Indians he hired as guides) proceeded to paddle about 2700 kilometres in 20 days (starting out most mornings at 4:00 AM)! Mackenzie told me that it was nearly 1700 miles, and I have done the math to convert it to kilometres—one day this great land will use civilized units of measurement like France does.

FEB. 1, 1793—STILL WAITING FOR SPRING AT FORT FORK

There are plenty of willing distractions, because about 70 Indians live in this area. Although of rather meagre appearance, some of the women are *trés jolie,* as we say in Montréal. But Mackenzie is a strict master and will not let us "co-mingle" as he puts it. I am not surprised. The other day I made a little joke to the rest of our party: "The Spanish enslave the Indians, the British drive them out and the French marry them!" There were great gales of laughter, and Baptist Bisson said, "It's funny because it's true," but Mackenzie just went very red in the face and said he had to go and polish his sextant.

APR. 25, 1793—FORT FORK

Well, we are still here, but the good news is that today the ice on the river finally broke, and we shall be able to get underway soon. I think I have finally figured out Mackenzie—he is one of those people who realize that if you're bossy enough, eventually you'll find people who like it and will stick to you like flies to honey. Mackenzie's second in command, Alexander Mackay, seems to be particularly in the thrall of the chief. A few days ago I actually witnessed Mackay present Mackenzie with a *flower!* Admittedly it was done in the spirit of scientific observation, but this sort of thing really does not instill the rest of us with a sense of virile authority.

MAY 10, 1793

We finally set off yesterday on our voyage (at *4 o'clock in the morning* of course!) and already the seams of our birchbark canoe have started to leak because we are so heavily laden. Although our canoe is very light and strong, it is also very fragile. We have stopped now to plug the leaks by building a fire, boiling tree sap (which we carry with us) and then daubing it on the seams to seal the leaks. The men who were on Mackenzie's previous voyage told me that sometimes this will happen several times in a day and that some days more time is spent on shore fixing the canoe than actually paddling! What sort of adventure is this? I decided to sneak off behind a tree to write this journal entry.

And another thing—Mackenzie has spent the whole winter going on and on about how he went to London to study navigation after his last voyage. He drills it into our heads that he is the only one of us who knows how to navigate—and what does he do this morning? He drops his compass into the water and watches as it sinks into the murky depths. Luckily, it was just his pocket compass, and he still has his larger one, but heaven help us if this is the man leading us onward!

JUNE 5, 1793

Things are not going well—we have been nearly killed by landslides, we crash the canoe into rocks on an almost daily basis and must stop to fix it, and then once we have launched it, we crash it again almost immediately afterward. Many days, when the rapids of the river are too violent to pass, we must unload the canoe (1500 kilos worth of supplies) and lug them overland (we carry about 40 kilos each, and two of us must also carry the canoe). Or if this is not practical, we unload the canoe and carry the supplies while we try to float the canoe through the most violent waters by means of dragging it from shore with ropes.

Furthermore, I am convinced that Mackenzie has no idea where we are going. Today he actually *climbed a tree* to look around to see if he could figure out where we are. When the tree did not afford him enough of a view, he decided to go climb a nearby hill to see what he could see. This left me and some of the others to drag the canoe through a particularly hazardous stretch of whitewater. Of course, we broke the canoe on some rocks almost immediately and had to stop to fix it. The repairs took quite some time. Mackenzie had said he would fire his gun several times to give us a bearing on his location.

But we were so tired from repairing the canoe that we ignored the shots when we heard them. We also ignored the tree branches that he sent back down-river as a signal to us that he was upcurrent and that was where we could find him. We had a nap instead. We caught up with the rest of the party later in the day and simply told Mackenzie that the repairs to the canoe had taken a long time. He plainly did not believe us, but said nothing.

June 11, 1793

We met some Indians today, and Mackenzie decided to ask them for directions. Did they know if there was a river that leads directly to the ocean? The Indian chief asked why Mackenzie needed to ask him at all, because, didn't white men know everything in the world? Mackenzie hemmed and hawed and finally said that he knew where the ocean was and he knew our present location, but he did not know what lay between. I thought this was at least a truthful answer, and the Indians seemed satisfied, too. But later on, Mackenzie stood before us, pompously recounting the story and said, "Thus I fortunately preserved the impression in their minds of the superiority of white people over themselves." What an ass this man is!

June 12, 1793

The canoe is now so heavy from being patched and repaired that two of us can barely carry it 100 metres before we have to put it down and rest. This morning we were carrying the canoe and our

40-kilo packs through a swampy area where we sank into foul muck up to our knees, at which point a veritable plague of black flies descended upon us and began to feast on our blood. With the canoe held over our heads, we could not even swat the little devils away. Finally, out of desperation (now being very muddy and itchy), we put the canoe in the water, loaded it up and tried to paddle for a while, but no sooner were we afloat than the canoe was abruptly sucked into the irresistible current of the rapids ahead—we were spun round and round and thrown to and fro like a cork in a boiling pot! The canoe was smashed in half on some rocks, and we were lucky to escape with our lives.

After we had all gotten safely ashore, we were very shaken, but Mackenzie made us hike downriver to recover the halves of the canoe and what supplies we could. Then he insisted that we glue the two halves of the canoe back together, and at this point I resolved to speak my mind. "Are you mad? The canoe will be so heavy that it will break under its own weight and we shall have to build a new one. Let us simply build a new one now and start making our return journey."

"Our return journey?" said Mackenzie. "We are not returning. We must continue until we have reached the ocean."

"Are you mad?" I repeated. "Why should we continue when it is perfectly obvious that there is no route that gives us a practical way to get to the ocean—can you seriously imagine doing this laden with furs? We would lose all of the pelts through misadventures like we had today."

"There are more reasons to blaze new trails than for simple commerce," he said.

"What on earth do you mean?" I snapped.

"Even now we are depleting the stock of beaver in the Hudson basin through over-trapping, and eventually, the demand for beaver fur will subside," he replied.

"Over-trapping!?" I burst out. "What sort of mad talk is this? The supply of beavers is endless! One cannot hunt a species to extinction—such a thing is impossible. We will never run out of beavers!"

"It has already begun to happen," he said through clenched teeth. "That is why we have had to push farther and farther inland—to look for new trapping grounds and new Indians to trade with."

I had nothing to say to this for, when I stopped to think about it, he did appear to make sense—the beaver population *did* seem to be in decline.

"Very well," I conceded, "but the idea that one day people will no longer want hats made from beaver pelts is ludicrous! There will always be a demand for beaver-skin hats!"

"It doesn't matter how useful or popular something is," Mackenzie riposted. "Eventually, everyone will have all the hats they need, and even if we make new ones, no one will want to buy them."

This also seemed to make sense when I thought about it, but Mackenzie could see I was still doubtful and continued.

"Suppose someone were to invent something undeniably useful such as, let us say, a horseless self-propelling carriage of some sort."

"A horseless, self-propelling carriage? How would that even work?"

"I don't know," said Mackenzie, "but the point is that you cannot deny its usefulness—everyone who could afford one would want one."

"Of course," I agreed.

"Very well then, but now imagine that after years and years of producing such a thing, everyone who can afford a horseless carriage has one, and no matter how badly they are built, they simply do not break down fast enough for people to need to keep buying new ones. But instead of recognizing this, we continue to make more horseless carriages—now we have a product that no one wants to buy. Let us further suppose that in order to propel itself, the horseless carriage requires some sort of fuel, let us say—"

"—a viscous oozing oil that comes out of the ground!" piped in Baptist Bisson.

"Fine," said Mackenzie. "Now let us further suppose that it is very expensive to extract this oil and that there is not an endless supply of it either."

I began to see what he was getting at. "In that case, you would have a product that was very expensive to make for which there was no demand and that required equally expensive, yet finite, raw materials to maintain."

"And that, gentlemen, is the current predicament we fur traders find ourselves in regarding hats made from beaver pelts. It affects you too."

Baptist Bisson piped up again. "You mean we won't always be well paid for performing the same repetitive task over and over again?"

"Perhaps not," said Mackenzie. "And so you can see that although the purpose of this trip is ostensibly to discover whether it is practical to trade with Indians on the west coast, more important than that, we must push on to explore the land that lies between—who knows what new possibilities may lie there."

"So we're on a quest for something, but we don't know what it is," I said.

"We do know where we are going though, and that is to the ocean," replied Mackenzie firmly.

After this I determined to follow Mackenzie with as much devotion as the next man. Now that he has explained the lay of the land as it were, I realize that it really doesn't matter if we do not know exactly where we are, because that must be expected when one is exploring a new world!

WHAT'S REAL

Jacques Beauchamp and Baptist Bisson were part of Mackenzie's crew, as were Joseph Landry, Charles Ducette and Alexander Mackay. However, Mackenzie is the only member of the expedition who is known to have kept a journal, and Jacques Beauchamp is only mentioned twice: once when Mackenzie lists the names of his crew, and again on June 12 when he writes that Beauchamp did not want to continue.

For the most part, the events described took place and, usually, on the dates I have indicated. I have made up Mackenzie's thick Scottish accent (he was born in Scotland but his family came to the New World when he was 10), Beauchamp's general lechery as well as the joke that he tells on Feb. 1 (though it is a reasonable summary of Aboriginal–European relations at the time), and the entire conversation that took place on June 12, 1793.

It is obvious from Mackenzie's journals that up to the end, and even on the return trip, most of his men were sick and tired of the extremes they were expected to endure. And finally, what is truly missing from this short account is the ongoing series of encounters Mackenzie had with First Nations groups, some of whom were happy to see him and some of whom were decidedly not.

THIRTEEN

The Curious Case
of John Fubbister

Since 1968, As It Happens *has been the CBC's pre-eminent phone-out show. The producers place a call to any place on earth that has a phone and a breaking news story. The stories range from harrowing interviews with correspondents whose lives may be in imminent danger, to quirky light-hearted stories of local interest. The show also maintains the eccentric habit of pinpointing some callers' locations as being so many miles from Reading, a town in the south of England. If radio (and* As It Happens*) had existed in 1807, the following call certainly would have been a surprising one. We join the call in progress with host Marilou Finley…*

MARILOU: On the line with us tonight is Alexander Henry, the factor of the North West Company's post at Pembina on the shores of the Red River in Rupert's Land, one day to be known as Manitoba. Mr. Henry, good evening.

ALEXANDER: Salutations, Marilou.

MARILOU: For our listeners at home, what exactly does a *factor* do at a fur-trading post? It's a job that not all of our listeners may be familiar with.

ALEXANDER: A factor is the company's official agent at a given site, and so I enjoy the duty of being the North West Company's representative here.

MARILOU: I see. Now, I understand that your archrival, the Hudson's Bay Company, has a post nearby, is that right?

ALEXANDER: Your supposition is correct, though I should hasten to point out that the rivalry between our firms does not prevent us from celebrating the advent of the New Year at one another's posts. A bit of companionship goes a long way in these remote environs, even among archrivals, as you put it.

MARILOU: I understand that's what was happening last week?

ALEXANDER: That is also correct. We had a group of the Hudson's Bay men here for a bit of jollification over the holidays. It has become quite a tradition for them to come to our post for a visit at this time of year.

MARILOU: So far so good. What happened next?

ALEXANDER: Among their party was a young lad by the name of John Fubbister. The other HBC men were of the opinion that young Fubbister was a good egg and worked hard and well just like the rest of them. He seemed to be well liked, and his fellow colleagues told me that he had signed on with them in the Orkney Islands just off the northern coast of Scotland.

MARILOU: The Orkneys are about 700 miles from Reading, is that right?

ALEXANDER: That is correct, though I fail to see what that has to do with anything.

MARILOU: It doesn't.

ALEXANDER: If you'll let me continue…Fubbister's companions told me that after a three-week crossing of the Atlantic Ocean, the ship he was on had arrived at the HBC's Moose Factory post, which, as you know, is quite a remote location.

MARILOU: As a matter of fact, it's 3267 miles from Reading.

ALEXANDER: If you are quite done, I shall continue. As I was saying, for the next year and a half, this young Fubbister seemed to have worked hard and earned his keep. He laboured on several long and arduous journeys delivering goods up and down the length of the Albany River and finally completing a trip of nearly 1000 miles to the HBC fort here.

MARILOU: All in canoes and small open boats?

ALEXANDER: That is correct. Now, on December 29 of this year, the HBC contingent was here at our fort for their customary celebrations, and after many a good bottle, they were preparing to return to their own post for the night when this Fubbister lad said that he felt unwell and asked if he could stay behind. I was surprised at the fellow's demand; however, I told him to sit down and warm himself.

I returned to my own room, where I had not been long before he sent one of my people, requesting the favour of speaking with me. Accordingly I stepped down to him and was much surprised to find him extended out upon the hearth, uttering most dreadful lamentations. He stretched out his hand toward me and, in a pitiful tone of voice, begged my assistance and requested that I take pity upon a poor, helpless abandoned wretch—who was not of the sex I had every reason to suppose but was an unfortunate Orkney girl pregnant and actually in childbirth. In saying this, she opened her jacket and displayed to my view a pair of beautiful white round breasts!

MARILOU: John Fubbister is a woman?!

ALEXANDER: With beautiful white round breasts, yes.

MARILOU: How is that possible? How could a woman conceal her true sex from men she had worked in close quarters with for more than a year?

ALEXANDER: The Hudson's Bay Company is keeping very tight-lipped about the whole thing, but it seems to me that at least some of the other HBC men must have known her secret and kept it to themselves.

MARILOU: Do we know who the father of the child is?

ALEXANDER: The overwhelming suspicion is that the father is a man named John Scarth who sailed on the same voyage that brought this Fubbister character from the Orkney Islands to the New World.

Alexander Henry gets a surprise.

There's even some talk that she may have been in love with him back in the Orkneys and so embarked on this desperate masquerade in order to stay close to him.

MARILOU: But isn't it also possible that she liked the idea of earning £8 a year in the guise of a man, which is more than she could earn as a woman at any other honest profession?

ALEXANDER: That is a distinct possibility.

MARILOU: And who is this person? What is her name?

ALEXANDER: For a while the HBC took to calling her Mary Fubbister, but now they call her Isabel Gunn.

MARILOU: Is that her real name?

ALEXANDER: No one knows.

MARILOU: And how is her baby doing?

ALEXANDER: Her son is doing fine.

MARILOU: What will happen to Ms. Gunn now?

ALEXANDER: It's against HBC policy to have white women at their posts, so she'll probably get shipped back to the Orkneys.

MARILOU: Why shouldn't she be allowed to continue doing the work she did before?

ALEXANDER: Besides having a child to care for, everyone knows that Canada is no place for a woman.

MARILOU: It's not?

ALEXANDER: Yourself excepted, of course, Marilou.

MARILOU: And with that, we're out of time. Mr. Henry, thank you for talking with us tonight.

ALEXANDER: It's been a pleasure.

WHAT'S REAL

The paragraph in which Alexander Henry describes his discovery of John Fubbister's secret is nearly a verbatim quote from his journal entry covering the event. His description of the Hudson's Bay Company's reaction is also accurate but is not a direct quote. Not much is known of Isabel Gunn's fate after this. She and her son returned to the Hudson's Bay post the same day he was born, and in the spring of 1808 they both returned to Fort Albany. Here, the HBC actually honoured the terms of her contract until it ended in 1809, continuing to pay her £8 per year, but for performing the work of a washerwoman instead of a labourer.

Isabel Gunn may also have worked as a nurse at the post's newly opened school. Although she did not want to return to the Orkneys, the HBC shipped her and her son back home where her fate is unknown. Some accounts say she found work as a "stocking and mitten" maker and that she died in 1861 at the age of 81. In spite of the HBC's mixed treatment of her in 1807, today she has been rehabilitated into a folk hero and is described in HBC literature as their first "female adventurer."

FOURTEEN

The Earl of Selkirk's Excellent Misadventures (1805–18)

In the early 19th century, Thomas Douglas Selkirk, the fifth Earl of Selkirk, sponsored a series of attempted settlement schemes to populate Canada. If so many people hadn't died so unpleasantly, and if Lord Selkirk's good intentions had been bolstered by something more than staggering indifference and oblivious incompetence, it might have actually been funny. He clearly considered himself an expert on colonizing, but since he does not appear to have written a "How to" guide on the subject, I have taken the liberty of doing so for him.

Lord Selkirk's

DO-IT-YOURSELF GUIDE TO
SETTLING CANADA

INTRODUCTION

SETTLING A NEW COUNTRY can be a daunting undertaking—but not if you're independently wealthy and blessed with a peculiar

☞

mixture of practical knowledge and utter cluelessness (like I am). I should also point out that when I say "Do-it-yourself," what I really mean is "Supply-all-the-money-and-land-but-hire-other-people-to-do-the-work-for-you." When things get bad, it also helps to completely ignore the bad news, and when you are embroiled in any sort of argument or dispute (especially over land claims), simply assume that you are always in the right. Armed with those few pointers, I think you are now ready to embark on that most exciting of adventures—settling Canada yourself!

The Basics

The first thing that any country needs in order to be settled is…settlers! A good way to get settlers is to find some disadvantaged group of people whose lives are so abysmal that damnation itself seems preferable to the squalid misery of their daily toil. Wretches such as these are ideal candidates for citizenship in Canada, though they will likely regret the decision once they arrive. In my case, I was lucky enough to be Scottish, during a time when the Highland variety of my fellow Scots were being cleared off their

☞

land to make grazing grounds for hundreds of thousands of English sheep. This made me so angry that I decided I would find homes for them (and their sheep), even if it meant displacing some other group of hapless unfortunates. There's an old saying where I come from: "If they're no' Scottish, they're crap!"

The second thing you will need to do is to buy up a controlling interest in some huge private landowner, such as the Hudson's Bay Company. It also doesn't hurt if your wife's brother sits on the governing committee of that same huge private landowner. If you can carve out (or better yet, marry into) a situation like this, then you can wield a great deal of influence with practically no accountability. The world—or more specifically, Canada—is your oyster! Admittedly, it is an oyster with very cold winters and, in some parts, regrettably prone to flooding, but more on that later!

The third and perhaps most important quality for a wannabe settler of Canada to possess is perseverance. Even when your first two attempts at colonizing Canada have failed miserably with considerable loss of life, whatever you do, don't try to learn from your mistakes—learning from your mistakes will just slow you down when you're climbing back on to your lame, elderly, poorly shod horse to make your next set of mistakes. Hi Yo, Silver!

How to Settle in Ontario, 1804–18

There are things we know that we know—these are known knowns; these are things we know we know. We also know there are known unknowns; that is to say, we know there are some things we do not know. But there are also unknown unknowns—the ones we don't know we don't know. Smart men know this and will be saying it long after I am gone. Try to bear these words of wisdom in mind if you're planning to settle in Ontario.

Step 1: Find a nice plot of land somewhere (I called mine "Baldoon") and set to work with great energy making preparation for the arrival of your 15 families of settlers. Clear forested land for grazing cattle and sheep. Build a barn and 14 houses. Why 14 houses and not 15? I have no idea. Supply livestock and provisions for the first winter. Start planting crops.

Step 2: Fail to realize that your lovely, flat, arable land will flood in case of heavy rains. Actually, failing to realize this was Step 1, but this was one of the many things I did not know that I did not know at the time.

Step 3: Before you head back to England, hire a disinterested Toronto politician called Alexander McDonnell to look after things. McDonnell will only occasionally tear himself away from the centre of the universe—Muddy York—to come and check on things. Finally, not to be bothered, he'll simply hire an even less competent underling to do the job for him.

Step 4: Try to return home to England (wait a minute, am I not Scottish?) when the entire settlement floods, destroying all the crops and supplies and flooding the homes. When the mosquitoes bring the malaria, and 16 of your settlers die, you don't want to be anywhere nearby.

☞

Step 5: You might suppose that it can't possibly rain heavily two years in a row, so you might as well stay away for the second year, too. And you'd be right in that supposition—in fact, it doesn't rain at all, and there's a terrible drought. Now the heads of seven of the 15 families have also inconsiderately died. How unScottish of them.

Step 6: Petition the Government of Upper Canada to let your settlers relocate to nearby lands that are currently reserved for the First Nations. After all, the English did it to my settlers, so why shouldn't I do it to the Indians? When the government turns down your request, just keep trying, but it will be to no avail.

Step 7: When your still swampy settlement is captured by invading Americans during the War of 1812, then recaptured by the British and then retaken by the Americans, try to make sure that you're preoccupied with your new settlement in Manitoba.

☞

How to Settle in Manitoba, 1812–17

Step 1: Location, location, location! Pick a spot that satisfies your ulterior motives but is otherwise a completely insane place to expect people to live—by this I mean Winnipeg (or the location that will one day be known as Winnipeg). If a company you own a controlling interest in (such as the Hudson's Bay Company) has a rival with a legitimate licence to trade furs in your territory (such as the North West Company), plunk your settlers down right in the middle of their trade routes so you can disrupt their dealings with the local communities (such as the Métis) who have lived on "your" land for years.

Step 2: Once again, don't actually show up to do any of the work yourself (until it's too late). Once you've gotten the Hudson's Bay Company to grant you a huge tract of land where the Red and Assiniboine rivers meet, appoint a governor who's just as high-handed and arrogant as you are—by this I mean Miles MacDonnell.

Step 3: Make NO provisions to feed or shelter your settlers, but keep sending them year after year even though many of them die from scurvy, malnutrition and exposure. Continue to make NO provision for feeding or sheltering them.

Step 4: Once you've pissed off your local business rivals and the indigenous community, make matters worse by claiming that the food they make (by this I mean *pemmican*, the mixture of buffalo meat, fat, grains and berries that is a staple hereabouts) "belongs" to you because it was made on land that "belongs" to you as well. Refuse to purchase or trade this food since it "belongs" to you. Then, when your settlers are starving because of your own incompetence and indifference, lead a raid on the local warehouse to reclaim the food that was "rightfully yours" in the first place. Even if you yourself cannot be

☞

present to carry this out, make sure to empower your governor—Miles MacDonnell—to do it for you.

Step 5: Take action only after the following events have happened.

- Your rivals and their allies have routinely harassed your settlers and burnt down or destroyed their homes and forts.

- Many of your settlers have died from the causes listed in Step 3.

- As a result of high-handed, unilateral decisions made by your wacky governor, the Métis fight back, and their victory at the Battle of Seven Oaks defines them as a socio-political entity.

Step 6: The action you take should be as follows.

- Have yourself declared a Justice of the Peace in Canada (when in reality you are a delusional Little Lord Fauntleroy in a kilt).

- Hire 100 Swiss mercenaries (Meurons) and 100 voyageurs on

☞

top of that and lead them to your colony (when you arrive make sure that you are exhausted, sick and mentally unstable—not being accustomed to actually doing anything yourself).

- Once you arrive, arrest the head of the North West Company at his own fort and on no one's authority other than your own.

- Take him to Montréal for trial, but once there, stand trial yourself for conduct best described in legal terms as "utterly bonkers" and wind up paying £3000 in damages.

Step 7: Die (already) in 1820, your reputation in ruins and plagued by debt.

FINISHING TOUCHES

Rest assured that a few hardy settlers will stay on and that your colony of people struggling to survive on the prairie will one day grow to be a large city of people struggling to survive on the prairie.

WHAT'S REAL

Sadly, everything mentioned above did happen. To save space, I even left out Selkirk's failed colony of 800 people in PEI that was unfolding (or unravelling) at roughly the same time he was settling Baldoon.

In a few pages of flippant humour, it is impossible to convey the duration and degree of suffering that Lord Selkirk inflicted both on his settlers and on the people already living in the areas he attempted to colonize. Way to go, Hudson's Bay Company! Now just bring on some Bay Days and everything will be OK.

FIFTEEN

Franklin's Lost Expedition: The Prequel (1819–22)

Sir John Franklin is one of the most famous explorers of Canada, but for all the wrong reasons. His most famous voyage is the 1845 expedition from which he never returned. Along with his entire crew of 132 men, Franklin vanished into Canada's Arctic, never to be heard from again until graves with well-preserved frozen corpses began to be unearthed in the early 1980s. However, Franklin's lost expedition was actually his fourth to the Arctic and his third as commanding officer. Given how badly his first expedition turned out, it is puzzling that he was given another chance. If we'd had reality TV shows in the 1840s...

ANNOUNCER: *Last time on* Survival: Arctic Tundra—*Lieutenant Franklin gets his orders from Sir John Barrow!*

BARROW: Lieutenant Franklin, your orders are to proceed overland to Great Slave Lake. From there you will proceed to the arctic coast by way of

Sir John Franklin

---

the Coppermine River. Once at the coast, you will head back east to rendezvous with the ships of Rear Admiral Edward Parry, who by that time will have both discovered and navigated the North West Passage.

FRANKLIN: Yes, sir. You can count on me, sir. Relying on unlikely outcomes that are completely uncertain seems like a prudent plan to me. Whatever happens, I will stay the course.

ANNOUNCER: *But things get off to a bad start when Franklin's party arrives at York Factory on the southern shores of Hudson Bay. George Back, one of Franklin's men, breaks the bad news.*

BACK: Well, sir, you see, the thing is that the North West Company and the Hudson's Bay Company have both promised to give us supplies and men.

FRANKLIN: Yes, that's right, Back, but I don't see any men or supplies.

BACK: That's just the thing, sir. As it happens, the North West Company and the Hudson's Bay Company are currently involved in a pitched battle against one another for domination of the fur trade. They say they have not the time, resources nor inclination to be of any assistance to us.

FRANKLIN: Be that as it may, Back, we must stay the course.

BACK: But how will we stay the course without any supplies or men? It gets very cold here, you know.

FRANKLIN: We must stay the course, Back. We must stay the course.

ANNOUNCER: *Things go from bad to worse when Franklin chooses the balmy month of January to lead an advance party to Fort Chipewyan to hire voyageurs for the rest of the trip.*

BACK: Perhaps it would have been better if we had not brought so much tea with us and had instead brought some tents to protect us from the snow.

FRANKLIN: Nonsense, Back. Who needs tents when the snow itself forms an insulating layer on us as we sleep? And what Englishman can call himself an Englishman if he does not have his cup of tea?

BACK: It just seems like a bit of a luxury item compared to the necessities of survival—like tents. Besides, it's so cold that our tea freezes solid as soon as we pour it out of the pot.

FRANKLIN: Back, you know as well as I do that we have no way of actually knowing how cold it is.

BACK: Yes, because the mercury in the thermometer got so cold that it broke!

FRANKLIN: Listen, Back, just because we are completely inexperienced in harsh environments such as this one is no reason for us to shirk our duty to—

BACK: Let me guess—

FRANKLIN: Stay the course!

ANNOUNCER: *Franklin and his party of four naval personnel manage to hire 16 voyageurs, but they aren't very good. He sets up a new base called Fort Providence. There, he meets Akaitcho, the chief of the Yellowknife tribe who agrees to help the explorers if Franklin promises that the Yellowknives' debt to the North West Company will be erased (something that Franklin has no authority to grant).*

AKAITCHO: I am Akaitcho.

FRANKLIN: Bless you. Gesundheit.

AKAITCHO: We will hunt for you and leave food cached along your route even though you seem to have no idea what your route will be. But I must warn you that the winter is a harsh one, and even hunters as experienced as we may not be able to catch enough food to provide for you.

FRANKLIN: I acknowledge your dire and likely accurate warning, which I choose to ignore in favour of—staying the course!

ANNOUNCER: *Lieutenant Franklin tells us how he's doing.*

FRANKLIN: By choosing to ignore practical advice and my own lack of experience, wisdom or knowledge, I find it much easier to stay the course, even if I don't know what that course is or why I should work so hard at staying it. I think that makes me a strong leader.

ANNOUNCER: *Franklin's poorly equipped and unprepared party pushes on and pitches a new camp they call Fort Enterprise, but soon there's trouble in the ranks over a comely Indian lass named Greenstockings.*

BACK: I want her!

MIDSHIPMAN ROBERT HOOD: No, *I* want her.

FRANKLIN: Now, now, men, we must stay the course. And right now that means that I am sending you, Mr. Back, to return to Fort Providence and demand that they send us some supplies, for otherwise we shall die of starvation, even though we are staying the course.

BACK: You want me to make a 1200-mile journey on snowshoes, with nothing more than a blanket for shelter and in temperatures as low as –55°C? And then you want me to browbeat our so-called corporate benefactors into giving me supplies and then lug them all the way back while you sit here drinking tea and not doing anything?

FRANKLIN: Why, yes, Back, you've summed it up admirably. We must stay the course.

ANNOUNCER: *After Back gets back with the supplies weeks later, Franklin has to stave off mutiny as the starving voyageurs start dropping the canoes on sharp rocks.*

FRANKLIN: I say, men, stop dropping those canoes on those sharp rocks! I do believe you're doing it on purpose so that you don't have to carry them any more when they break. If I didn't know better, I would surmise that you are forming some kind of an alliance against me.

BACK: Sir, the men might be in a better mood if they'd had more than lichen to eat. You did promise them each eight pounds of meat a day, and as well as the canoes, they're carrying 90-pound packs.

FRANKLIN: Don't worry, Smithers—

BACK: The name's Back.

FRANKLIN: You see, the pangs of hunger will be lessened if we imagine that these insubstantial lichens on which we barely subsist are really a scrumptious feast. Perhaps if we were to call them *tripe de roche* instead.

BACK: Fat of the rocks?

FRANKLIN: Exactly. We shall stay the course.

BACK: Ah, look at that. The men have dropped the canoes again, and they're all broken. Looks like they're throwing away the fishing nets to lighten the load too.

ANNOUNCER: *For a while the voyageurs are glad they don't have to carry the canoes, but that changes when Franklin's party* finally *arrives at the mouth of the Coppermine River.*

FRANKLIN: At last! The Coppermine River. And look how wide it is and how swiftly the current moves. Well, men, we must stay the course and cross the river.

THE MEN: Hurrah! Hey, wait a minute, we don't have any canoes!

FRANKLIN: And you threw the nets away, too. Those would have come in handy right about now.

ANNOUNCER: *It's a death-defying moment as Franklin's men try to complete this week's challenge by using ropes to haul themselves across the 120-foot-wide river. But after everyone nearly drowns, they give up—the current is too fast and the distance too far. Finally, team member and interpreter Pierre St. German builds a small boat out of tree branches and canvas. It's a little leaky by* *the end of its voyage, but everyone gets across safely. And now, after the longest recap in history—this week on* Survival: Arctic Tundra—*the exploring party splits up when some of the men are too weak to continue.*

FRANKLIN: We're not doing too well, and although I try to keep my strength up, I wouldn't be surprised if we "get eliminated" so to speak.

BACK: I certainly wish we had immunity to cold, hunger and privation, but alas, we do not.

FRANKLIN: Our little tribe is splitting up—Mr. Hood and Mr. Richardson are too weak to continue, and so they shall stay behind at our current camp with Mr. Hepburn to look after them. Our hope is that we can return for them at some later date with the food they desperately need. I shall push on with nine of the voyageurs in the hopes of reaching Fort Enterprise, where Chief Akaitcho has promised to leave us food.

BACK: Yes, but he promised that months ago, and we know that it's been a rough winter, with little game for hunting.

FRANKLIN: Yes, but I am choosing to stake all of our hopes on that most unlikely of outcomes.

BACK: Which is that you have chosen once again to send me on ahead so that when I have reached Fort Enterprise, I can double-back to return with food.

FRANKLIN: As always, you have summed up the situation with clarity, Back. We must stay the course.

ANNOUNCER: *But right away, some of the voyageurs with Franklin switch allegiance—well, actually, they just lose heart and ask to go back to the camp where Hood, Richardson and Hepburn are staying.*

FRANKLIN: Very well. You men, Terohaute, Belanger, Perrault and Fontano, may return to our previous camp while I continue on with these five others.

ANNOUNCER: *Meanwhile, up ahead, there's a nasty surprise in store for George Back at Fort Enterprise.*

BACK: There's no food here! Well, I'm not surprised. Akaitcho probably assumed we'd never make it here alive and so didn't bother wasting good food on walking dead men. I shall leave a note for Franklin's party and push on ahead to Fort Providence to look for Akaitcho.

ANNOUNCER: *Back at camp, Hood, Richardson and Hepburn are surprised when Terohaute stumbles into camp alone.*

HOOD: What are you doing here?

TEROHAUTE: Er...well...Belanger, Perrault, Fontano and I split off from Franklin's party to come back, but I...uh...got separated from the others, and uh...I have all of this meat for you!

HOOD, RICHARDSON and HEPBURN: Meat?! Where did you get meat?! Lord Bless you, man, let's have at it.

TEROHAUTE: It's...er...*wolf* meat is what it is.

RICHARDSON: Who knew that wolves were so meaty?

HEPBURN: And so delicious!

HOOD: Now, now, men, we must be sure to save some for Belanger, Perrault and Fontano when they catch up.

TEROHAUTE: Oh, I wouldn't worry about that. They're beyond hunger now.

HOOD: What do you mean?

TEROHAUTE: Oh…nothing…just that there's plenty to go around.

ANNOUNCER: *But while his men back at camp are feasting on meat, out on the trail, Franklin and his party are forced to eat their own boots.*

FRANKLIN: The men say the taste of shoe leather is revolting, but I tell them to think of it as *filet of sole.*

ANNOUNCER: *There's also trouble back at camp where Terohaute is starting to behave erratically.*

TEROHAUTE: Why should I collect *tripe de roche* when we are so well fed with meat?

HOOD: Then perhaps you wouldn't mind going hunting.

TEROHAUTE: No, I shall not, for there are no animals to hunt in this area. You had better eat *me* instead.

RICHARDSON: What are you on about?

TEROHAUTE: I do believe that you Britons have eaten my uncle!

HEPBURN: He's gone off his rocker.

ANNOUNCER: *Hepburn and Richardson discuss their concerns about Terohaute.*

HEPBURN: I think Terohaute murdered Belanger, Perrault and Fontano, and we've been feasting on their bodies.

RICHARDSON: Eewwwe! That's totally gross!

(Sound of gunshot is heard off-screen. The camera follows Robertson and Hepburn as they run along a trail through the woods where they come upon Terohaute holding a smoking gun over the dead body of Hood.)

TEROHAUTE: Hood was cleaning his gun and it accidentally went off!

RICHARDSON: Then why is the wound in the back of his head?

HEPBURN: And why does he have a book in one hand? Was he doing a little reading and cleaning his gun at the same time?

ANNOUNCER: *Next week on* Survival: Arctic Tundra...

RICHARDSON: I'm going to have to kill Terohaute before he kills us.

ANNOUNCER: *Franklin arrives at Fort Enterprise to find only a note from George Back saying that there is no food and he has gone to look for Chief Akaitcho. The food situation is dire by the time Richardson and Hepburn reach Fort Enterprise.*

FRANKLIN: Sorry, men, but we've had to eat the animal hides stretched over the windows. There's nothing left for you, and most of the other men are weeping wrecks who want nothing more than to die in peace. However, we must stay the course!

ANNOUNCER: *But just when things look darkest...*

FRANKLIN: Smithers! You've come back!

BACK: It's Back, sir. George Back. And I have brought men and supplies from Chief Akaitcho. You are saved!

ANNOUNCER: *Be sure to tune in next time for* Survival: Arctic Tundra*!*

—⟶⟵—

WHAT'S REAL

The main facts of this piece are all true. I have portrayed Franklin as slightly battier than he probably really was, but few historians dispute his staggering incompetence and inflexibility during changing circumstances. Although there is no evidence that he actually used the phrase "stay the course," a reference to George W. Bush's misguided adventures in Iraq, it seemed convenient shorthand to suggest pig-headed intransigence in the face of adverse circumstances.

The remarkable George Back later became an explorer in his own right and performed all of the heroic deeds described herein. Franklin's party called edible lichen tripe de roche, *but they probably did not use the phrase "filet of sole" in reference to eating their own shoe leather.*

Once he got back to England, Franklin was inexplicably celebrated as a hero, even though 11 of the 21 men on his expedition died—three were murdered by Terohaute; Terohaute himself was shot by Richardson, and seven more died from starvation. Franklin also travelled 8900 kilometres (5530 miles), having failed to explore the full extent of the coastline as he had been charged to do. And for all this he was made a hero and put in charge of further expeditions.

SIXTEEN

Our Space Invaders

Canada has been threatened by invasion from the U.S. on more than one occasion. What follows are three of the most significant, handily condensed into almanac form.

Ye Almanack for the Invasion of Canada
(with battle and weather predictions for the years 1775, 1812 and 1837)

1775

GENERAL PROGNOSTICATIONS: The year 1775 will see much ado in the United Colonies of North America. Tempestuous conditions arising in the south will at first spread northward, eventually receding due to circumstance, poor planning and apathy.

CAUSES: Understandable frustration with the oppressive British regime on the part of the Americans. A rapacious lust for land, also on the part of the Americans. The assumption, once again on the part of the Americans, that people who are not Americans want to become Americans.

BATTLE PREDICTIONS: Expect American invaders to attack Montréal and Québec in early December. These Yankee interlopers mistakenly believe that all of Canada (especially Québec) will want to join them in seceding from Britain. Don't worry though—by the time the invasion force arrives, it will likely have lost at least half its men as the result of disease, starvation and desertion.

PRACTICAL HINTS: Trying to invade Canada (or indeed any country) by leading an untrained, ill-equipped army over several hundred miles of rugged terrain during winter is not advised. Also, expecting to be welcomed as liberators is a dicey supposition in any century and on any continent.

WHAT YOU CAN DO: If you are French Canadian, stay neutral and openly sell supplies to both the British and French forces. For entertainment, see if you can make out the gob-smacked expressions on the faces of the Americans when you do not join them in attacking your own country. If you are British, mount a defence consisting of professionally trained troops and drive out the invaders.

THINGS TO LOOK OUT FOR: When the Americans realize you do not want to join them, they will attack and pillage your homesteads under the assumption that murderously assaulting your family will make you want to become one of them. Expect Montréal to temporarily fall to American forces.

WEATHER PREDICTIONS: A heavy blizzard on or around December 4 will confuse the invaders who are already in unfamiliar territory. It will aid in the thumping defeat inflicted on the would-be "liberators" by the British forces at Québec. The snow will be so heavy that some of the invaders' bodies will not be revealed until the spring thaw.

PREDICTED OUTCOMES: On or around July 2, the insurgents will withdraw from Canada and two days later will attempt to legitimize their terrorist invasion by drafting a "Declaration of Independence."

1812

GENERAL PROGNOSTICATIONS: 1812 will see the beginning of unfavourable and severe conditions that will last for the next two years. A transAtlantic political system will cause the collision of two fronts, with violent outbreaks stemming partly from conditions in the Atlantic and spreading inland.

CAUSES: Understandable frustration with the oppressive British regime on the part of the Americans. A rapacious lust for land, also on the part of the Americans. The assumption, once again on the part of the Americans, that people who are not Americans want to become Americans.

BATTLE PREDICTIONS: Expect a mixture of heavy fighting and light skirmishes as the War of 1812 progresses. Major or decisive battles will include:

- the capture of Detroit (by the British and Iroquois)
- the capture of York/Toronto (by the Americans)
- the Battle of Châteauguay (a victory for Canadian forces, the British leaving them to their own devices)
- the Battle of Chrysler's farm (a defeat for the Americans)
- the Battle of Lundy's Lane (both sides claim victory)
- the burning of Washington (by the British)
- the standoff at Plattsburgh (in which the Americans face down a much larger British force)
- the Battle of New Orleans (won by the Americans, but the war will have technically ended already)

HOUSEHOLD HINTS: This one's for the Americans—if British forces have set fire to the president's home and you are faced with stubborn stains from smoke damage, you may find that a good coat of whitewash will brighten up the place, and then you can call it the White House.

WHAT YOU CAN DO: Be vigilant of surprise attacks by the Americans. For example, if American soldiers commandeer your home and foolishly discuss plans for a surprise attack on Beaver Dams right in front of you, then walk for

32 kilometres—especially if you are a homesteader named Laura Secord—to warn the combined British and Mohawk forces who will then foil the attack.

THINGS TO LOOK OUT FOR: If you are part of the Iroquois and First Nations confederacy led by Tecumseh (allied with the British), be forewarned that once General Brock is dead, you will have no advocate. The British and Canadians are going to sell your asses up the river to the Americans and let them steal all the rest of your land.

WEATHER PREDICTIONS: Nothing much is going to happen during the winter months because the Americans don't do winter wars. Expect most major or decisive engagements to take place between early spring and late autumn.

PREDICTED OUTCOMES: The Americans will rarely win on the battlefield, but in a spineless betrayal of their First Nations allies, Britain will nonetheless cede to the U.S. lands previously reserved as an "Indian Buffer Zone." The idea of Aboriginal autonomy will become a thing of the past. Aside from this, the borders in place before the war revert to their previous positions. North of the border, some inhabitants of the British colonies will start to think of themselves as neither British nor American but *Canadian*.

1837

GENERAL PROGNOSTICATIONS: In Lower Canada (Québec), French Canadians (calling themselves *patriotes*) will engage in armed rebellion against the Château Clique, an appointed group of mainly anglo merchants and stakeholders who govern an assembly of democratically elected French Canadians. Louis-Joseph Papineau will emerge as the charismatic firebrand whose zeal others will follow. In Upper Canada (Ontario), English-speaking Canadians will engage in armed rebellion against the Family Compact, a group of wealthy landowners and merchants who are mainly Protestant. William Lyon Mackenzie will emerge as their ideological leader. Both rebellions will encourage some American elements to believe that once again Canada is ready to become a republic, and the time may be ripe for an invasion.

CAUSES: Understandable frustration with the oppressive British regime on the part of both French and English Canadians. A rapacious lust for land on the part of the Americans. The assumption, once again on the part of the Americans, that people who are not Americans want to become Americans.

BATTLE PREDICTIONS: In Lower Canada, look for some English Canadians (most notably Dr. Wolfred Nelson) to throw their support behind the *patriotes*, inciting the Battle of St. Denis. Here, the *patriotes* will kill six British soldiers and capture a cannon but will be routed two days later as the resurgent British forces kill 60 *patriotes* and arrest dozens more. British forces subsequently kill 100 more *patriotes* during the Battle of St. Eustache, effectively crushing the uprising. In Lower Canada, observers can expect an abortive rebel march down Yonge Street, which disintegrates after the opposing sheriff's forces fire a single volley. The next day, 1500 government reinforcements mop up the leftovers.

HOUSEHOLD HINTS: Dr. Wolfred Nelson's fiery exhortation, "The time has come to melt our spoons into bullets!" should not be taken literally. With the exception of silver, the metals that spoons are typically made of (pewter and steel) are utterly impractical for making bullets. While one certainly could melt silver into bullets, unless the opposing forces are made up of werewolves (*loup-garou* for the *patriotes*), this would be a serious waste of a valuable commodity.

WHAT YOU CAN DO: Pick a side.

THINGS TO LOOK OUT FOR: After the Battle of St. Eustache, Wolfred Nelson's brother, Robert, will establish a base in the U.S., leading raids over the border with support of American "Hunting Lodges" whose members want to create a sister republic in Canada. More people will be killed during these attempted invasions than in either of the original rebellions.

WEATHER PREDICTIONS: Cold weather usually has a way of dampening rebels' fiery spirits, but even though it will be December, Mackenzie may still manage to muster 500 locals armed with clubs, axes, pointed sticks and rifles. However, the sheriff's force of 25 men should manage to drive them off, the rebels not exactly being a disciplined fighting unit.

PREDICTED OUTCOMES: Compared to other rebellions, only a handful of deaths will occur. All of the prolonged unrest will prompt the previously unresponsive government in England to seriously consider the idea of "responsible government"; that is, giving Canadians more autonomy over their own governance.

WHAT'S REAL

All of the events happened, but of course, as with all brief summaries of this sort, the people involved and the situations they found themselves in were much more complicated. There were obviously many other players and influences than the few names mentioned. And finally, as a patriotic Canadian, this writer will not deny a degree of bias.

SEVENTEEN

Rose Fortune

Combining two different historical threads into one, here we imagine what might have happened if Rose Fortune had appeared on Front Page Challenge. *Rose Fortune was (among other things) arguably Canada's first black female law-enforcement representative, albeit self-appointed. She lived from 1774 to 1864.*

Front Page Challenge *was a weekly current events program that ran on CBC television from 1957 to 1995. A panel of three or four journalists would try to guess the identity of a mystery guest by asking him or her a series of leading questions. The mystery guest was always involved in some sort of newsworthy event, and his or her identity was revealed to the audience at the outset—the fun came from watching the panelists try to figure out who was sitting behind them. Some readers may also notice a resemblance to Canadian broadcaster Patrick Watson's series,* Witness to Yesterday *and* Titans *in which he conducted modern interviews with actors portraying notable figures from history.*

Front Page Challenge

Host: Fred Davidson

Challenger: Rose Fortune

Panelists: Gordon Éclair, Betty Kennealy, Pierre Merton

ANNOUNCER: *Ladies and Gentlemen, the "Man From Plaid" himself, Gordon Éclair.*

(Applause)

ANNOUNCER: *Not only smart, but smartly turned out, Betty Kennealy.*

(Applause)

ANNOUNCER: *Finally, a man whose bowtie never quits, Pierre Merton.*

(Applause)

FRED: And I'm your host, Fred Davidson. Well, panel, it looks like you're all ready to go, so let's tell the studio audience and the viewers at home who tonight's challenger is.

ANNOUNCER: *In the early 1800s, Rose Fortune became the first black woman in Canada to go into law enforcement. Working as a baggage porter on the shipping docks of Annapolis Royal, Nova Scotia, she appointed herself constable and kept order on the docks. Later she started her own overland shipping business that her descendants would continue until the 1960s. In 1984, one of her descendants, Daurene Lewis, became the first black woman in North America to become a mayor, when the residents of Annapolis Royal voted her into office.*

(Applause)

FRED: Gordon, the first round of questions goes to you.

GORDON: Are you a historical figure or modern-day?

ROSE: I don't know that you'd say I'm historic, but I'm from the past.

GORDON: Are you living or dead?

ROSE: Dead.

GORDON: Does your story have something to do with politics, business, sports or entertainment?

ROSE: I suppose politics and business come closest, but there's more to it than that.

GORDON: Civil or human rights then?

ROSE: That's what they call it nowadays.

GORDON Did the key events of your story happen in North America?

ROSE: Yes.

GORDON Does your story relate to the Underground Railroad that brought slaves to Canada in the 1860s?

ROSE: Yes, partly.

GORDON: Are you Harriet Tubman, black activist and helper of escaped slaves to freedom?

ROSE: No.

GORDON: Then, Betty, I'm handing it over to you.

BETTY: Are you Mary Ann Shadd, abolitionist, activist and anti-segregationist?

ROSE: No.

BETTY: Were you active on the west coast of North America?

ROSE: No.

BETTY: The east coast then?

ROSE: Yes.

BETTY: Were you ever a slave?

ROSE: No, my parents were freeborn black loyalists who fled to Canada.

FRED: A reminder, only yes or no answers.

ROSE: Oops—sorry.

BETTY: Did you help slaves?

ROSE: Later on.

BETTY: Later on? Well, Pierre, I'm out of time. It's up to you.

PIERRE: Were you in business for yourself before the time in your life when you began helping slaves?

ROSE: Yes.

PIERRE: Did you work on shipping docks as a porter and then as a policewoman?

ROSE: Yes.

PIERRE: Are you Rose Fortune, Canada's first policewoman and probably the first black police-woman in North America?

ROSE: Yes!

(Applause)

FRED: Well done, Pierre. Now, what do you think the headline would be?

PIERRE: Rose Fortune Breaks Down Barriers.

FRED: Correct.

(Applause)

FRED: Pierre, as the panelist who correctly guessed our challenger's identity, the first question goes to you.

PIERRE: Miss Fortune—is that correct—Miss Fortune?

ROSE: It sounds like you're saying "misfortune"— but, yes, that is correct.

PIERRE: Nowadays, Canadians in particular seem to regard Canada during your lifetime as less tolerant of slavery than the U.S. Would you say that was true?

ROSE: Partly. Don't forget, there was slavery in Canada even after the Act Against Slavery in 1793. Slave owners could still keep their slaves until they died. But toward the end of my life in 1864, yes, Canada was definitely the place to get to, though there was still a lot of prejudice.

PIERRE: Then and now, Miss Fortune. Then and now.

BETTY: How did you come to be a policewoman? Especially back then.

ROSE: Well, I wasn't an official police person in a hat and all that. How it started was that I had a business, carrying people's luggage for them when they were getting on and off the boats. I had a wheelbarrow and I'd load all their bags and trunks into it and take them to wherever they needed to go. But, like you'd expect, the docks were a tough place to be, and so after a while, the more nervous travellers wanted someone to escort them through the streets and so I started doing that. And then I got the idea of having a curfew to keep all the troublemakers off the docks after a certain time. Of course, there was no one but me to enforce that, and so that was how it started. I didn't have a uniform, though, if that's what you're thinking. I had a man's coat that I'd wear over my dress, because it was chilly down at the docks, and sometimes I had a stick that I'd whack the bad boys with if they didn't get out of my way.

BETTY: The boys?

ROSE: Oh, yes—the troublemakers on the docks weren't what you'd call "men"—they were mainly boys of what you might call the wayward variety. Sometimes they just wanted to horn in on my business, but a whack with a good stick can be the flail of salvation for a bad boy.

BETTY: Are you suggesting that—

FRED: Moving on to you, Gordon!

GORDON: Miss Fortune, we have a saying during my lifetime: "Where there is an open mind, there will always be a frontier." And my question is, did you know you were breaking down barriers when you were alive?

ROSE: Uh…it was more that I needed a job, and so I started doing what people were willing to pay me to do, which was carrying their luggage and keeping the docks peaceful. Then, later, they were willing to pay me to cart their luggage around with a horse and cart, and that was when I started my overland shipping business. I guess you could say that toward the end of my life—when I gave shelter to the folks who came up on what you call the Underground Railroad—that, yes, I knew it was something a bit different, but it was still something that just had to be done.

FRED: Well, our time is up, so thank you to our panelists and, of course, thank you to our challenger today, Rose Fortune.

(Applause)

WHAT'S REAL

So little is known about Rose Fortune that almost everything we do know is included in this section. A watercolour painting of her dated to 1830 shows a stockily built woman wearing a straw hat over a bonnet and a scarcely fitting man's overcoat over her dress. She is carrying a straw basket hooked over one arm and seems to be wearing sturdy, ankle-high boots.

One of the only surviving eyewitness accounts of Rose comes from later in her life when a Colonel Sleigh of the 77th Regiment was in Annapolis Royal in 1852 and apparently had some difficulty in getting out of a horrible inn that he had been visiting:

> I was aided in my hasty efforts to quit the abominable inn by a curious old Negro woman, rather stunted in growth…and dressed in a man's coat and felt hat; she had a small stick in her hand which she applied lustily to the backs of all who did not jump instantly out of the way. Poor old dame! She was evidently a privileged character.

EIGHTEEN

Mary Ann Shadd

Mary Ann Shadd (1823–93) was born in Delaware and moved around the U.S. before settling for a time in Toronto and marrying a Canadian. She returned to the U.S. after the death of her husband in 1861.

HERITAGE MCMOMENT #3

FROM: Richard Wanker
Broadcast Executive,
Historical TV Channel

TO: Mordant Wit
Freelance Writer

Greetings Mordant,

Welcome aboard once more for Heritage McMoment #3: "Mary Ann Shadd," the first woman to found, edit and publish a newspaper in Canada. I don't really understand the bit about how she "found" the newspaper—maybe back in those days you could start a newspaper if you just

☞

found one lying around? That might be an interesting thing to look into if you have time.

I've typed up the script for what we had in mind—I overheard our researcher here talking about Mary Ann, and I think he said she was a "demolitionist" or something. Can you please find out what a "demolitionist" is? It might be important, and I've put it into the script even though I have no idea what it means. I couldn't be bothered to ask the researcher even though he was right beside me—I was afraid I might look stupid. I know, I know—you're thinking to yourself, "How could anyone ever think a TV broadcast executive was stupid?" Well, you'd be surprised.

I also can't help but wonder if this story was where they got the idea for Mary Ann in *Gilligan's Island*. Can you look into that, too, please?

Sincerely,
Richard (Dick) Wanker

Heritage McMoment #3:
Mary Ann Shadd

Suggestions for visuals: I figure we show a woman either writing or delivering newspapers, or whatever it is that you do when you found, edit and publish a newspaper.

(Mary Ann is dressed like a woman of the 1850s— whenever that was. She works away at publishing her paper when a man bursts into the room.)

MAN

Why, you can't found, edit and publish a newspaper! You're a woman and a demolitionist to boot!

WRITER'S NOTES

Dick, although we've never met, I now truly believe that you are an illiterate sub-moron of drooling stupidity. Mary Ann Shadd was an ABOLITIONIST—someone who advocated ending (or abolishing) slavery. She herself was also black, and you might want to mention that in your directions. She was the daughter of freed slaves from the U.S. and was an important figure in the Underground Railway. While it is impressive, the fact that she was the first female newspaper publisher in Canada (her paper was called **The Provincial Freeman***) is not as important historically as her role in the anti-slavery movement.*

☞

MARY ANN SHADD

Yes, I can! I'll show you.

(Mary Ann starts working even harder at founding, editing and publishing her newspaper.)

Dick, for your information, when someone "founds" something, they are NOT finding it lying around in the road, but rather, they are starting some kind of undertaking or enterprise.

NARRATOR

In 1853, Mary Ann Shadd became the first woman in Canada to found, edit and publish a newspaper.

(Mary Ann is talking to some other women.)

MARY ANN SHADD

We have broken the "Editorial Ice" whether willingly or not, for your class in America, so go to editing as many of you who are willing and able, and as soon as you may, if you think you are ready.

Dick, it constantly baffles me as to how you can be such a slack-jawed half-wit at your job and still manage to find these quotes that actually fit the occasion. Do all the horseshoes clog up your toilet at all?

NARRATOR

Mary Ann Shadd—a great Canadian.

She was an American.

FROM: Richard Wanker
Broadcast Executive,
Historical TV Channel

TO: Mordant Wit
Freelance Writer

Hi Mordant,
   I asked my trusty assistant what
"illiterate submoron of drooling stupidity" means, and he says if I look at
the first letter of each word, it spells
"ISODS," which is the latest compliment
from the Internet or something—so
thanks!
   I thought your note about the Underground Railway was really interesting
because I didn't realize they had subways
back then—you know the craziest things!
   And thanks for explaining what an
"apologist" is. I was also really amazed
by what you said about her "starting
an undertaking or enterprise"—I can't
believe that, as well as finding, publishing and delivering her own newspaper (and being an apologist in her
spare time), she was also an undertaker!
That is so interesting. I didn't really
get the part about the *Enterprise*
though. The *Enterprise* is the name of

☞

the space ship in *Star Trek*, and what
I was asking about was *Gilligan's
Island*, which as you know, is another
great show from the 1960s. It's too bad
we don't have room for all of this in
the script, but finding the newspaper
is what's going to interest most people.

Looking forward to working on the
next Heritage McMoment with you: "When
Laurier Met Diefenbaker."

Sincerely,
Richard (Dick) Wanker

WHAT'S REAL

*Mary Ann Shadd was, of course, a real person and
was also a prominent abolitionist and participant in
the Underground Railway. When she published* The
Provincial Freeman, *it was in direct response to*
The Voice of the Fugitive, *a rival Toronto paper
published by Henry Bibb. Bibb was a former slave
who favoured racial segregation, while Mary Ann
Shadd was pro-integration.*

NINETEEN

Cornelius Krieghoff

Cornelius Krieghoff (1815–72) was a painter of Dutch heritage who settled in Canada. Although there had been plenty of sketches and paintings of the Canadian landscape up to this time, most of them had been done by military artists who were certainly capable but not necessarily inspired. Krieghoff was one of the first to interpret Canada's landscape with affection and artistry, at the same time imbuing it with a distinct personality. It is tempting to wonder what might have happened when he clashed with early patrons.

Cornelius Krieghoff

Appears on *Court TV: Small Claims Division*

©MDCCCXLIX(-ish)

(a transcript)

ANNOUNCER: *The plaintiff—Widow Lacroix—claims that she hired the defendant to paint her sitting room a rather ugly shade of beige but that instead he painted a mural of the view through her window.*

(The Widow Lacroix enters the courtroom and stands behind the dais.)

ANNOUNCER: *The defendant—artist and house-painter Cornelius Krieghoff—says he was hired to paint Widow Lacroix's wall, and that he painted her wall.*

(The defendant enters and stands in the dock.)

ANNOUNCER: *Presiding is Justice Eldridge Thackeray.*

(Justice Thackeray enters and sits.)

JUSTICE THACKERAY: Plaintiff, please state your case.

PLAINTIFF: I hired the defendant, Monsieur Krieghoff, to paint the walls of my living room. Nothing fancy. No murals. No rustic scenes showing a dramatic sky with a small, folksy cottage or domicile in the mid-ground. I didn't hire him to paint my portrait. I didn't hire him to paint a portrait of my neighbour's house. I didn't hire him to capture a moment in time as a team of horses pulled a sleigh past my icy windowsill. I hired him to paint my living-room walls a rather ugly shade of beige, which I happen to like.

JUSTICE THACKERAY: Defendant, how do you plead?

DEFENDANT: Not guilty, your Honour. It's true that the plaintiff hired me to paint the walls of her living room, but there were one or two other colours provided in addition to the rather ugly shade of beige.

PLAINTIFF: Oh, sure, there were other colours, but those were for the trim and the door frames.

JUSTICE THACKERAY: Madame Lacroix, did you specifically tell the defendant that the other paint was intended for that purpose?

PLAINTIFF: Well, no, but it's understood.

JUSTICE THACKERAY: Did you specifically tell the defendant that he was not to use the other colours in the painting of your walls?

PLAINTIFF: Well, no, but—

JUSTICE THACKERAY: Mr. Krieghoff, your name seems familiar and so does your face. Have we met before?

DEFENDANT: I believe we have, your Honour. There was a time when I was so desperate to sell my paintings that I went door-to-door with a selection of them offering them for sale.

JUSTICE THACKERAY: Why, yes, of course! I bought one!

PLAINTIFF: You were the only one, your Honour, so I thank you.

JUSTICE THACKERAY: It's a rather fetching study of some young men on a small flat sleigh being drawn across a snowy plain by a sturdy-looking steed while a dun-coloured winter sky lends an air of calm and stillness to the scene.

PLAINTIFF: What in the name of goodness is "dun"?

DEFENDANT: It's where grey meets brown.

PLAINTIFF: Not unlike…beige, perhaps?

JUSTICE THACKERAY: Exactly!

PLAINTIFF: Your Honour, you have just described almost to a tee the same picture the defendant painted on my wall, except that there's a rustic-looking house in the mid-ground with some tools visible in the yard.

JUSTICE THACKERAY: Ah, yes, mine has a cottage, too!

PLAINTIFF: So can we talk about my wall?

JUSTICE THACKERAY: More properly, we need to talk about the picture that the defendant has painted *on* your wall. Mr. Krieghoff—

DEFENDANT: Please, your Honour, call me Cornelius.

JUSTICE THACKERAY: Ah, excellent, well, then, Mr. Krieghoff—I mean, *Cornelius*—I don't believe I've ever encountered a painter so interested in Canada's landscape.

DEFENDANT: Well, yes, your Honour, I may very well be the first. But it's man's place within that landscape that inspired me, especially jolly moments during physical work and also, small cozy-looking buildings firmly in their place amid the wilds of Canada.

JUSTICE THACKERAY: What a charming choice of words.

PLAINTIFF: Speaking of small cozy buildings amid the wilds of Canada, my house is just such a building as you describe, and yet I do not find it is made any cozier by the scene that Mr. Krieghoff has painted on my wall. In fact, when I am *inside* my house, I would prefer not be constantly reminded of what may be happening *outside* my house. I live with rustic Canadian winters every year—the last thing I want is a painting of one.

JUSTICE THACKERAY: You know, Cornelius, sometimes I find that when the sky is overcast and the clouds are low, such as they are in many of your paintings, even when I am outside, I feel as though I am in a very large room with the clouds forming a gigantic ceiling. Do you ever feel that way?

DEFENDANT: Well, your Honour—

PLAINTIFF: Is this conversation really happening? Is there any chance that we could talk about my living room and not the emergence of a fledgling school of Canadian art?

JUSTICE THACKERAY: Very well, Madame Lacroix. You did not specifically tell the defendant not to use the other paints supplied when you directed him to paint your living room, and he certainly painted your living room. Therefore, I am ruling in favour of the defendant. Case dismissed. Now, *Cornelius*, perhaps I could interest you in a pot of ale along the street at the tavern?

WHAT'S REAL

Cornelius Krieghoff worked as a housepainter to support himself, and he reportedly tried hawking his paintings door-to-door. He is also famous for winter scenes such as the one described, and he revisited his favourite themes many times: people doing physical work in the Canadian wilderness; lone buildings or shelters in otherwise natural settings; winter sleigh rides; and nice horses, often combining some or all of these elements into one glorious yet folksy canvas.

There is no evidence that he ever painted a mural on someone's wall as described, and Widow Lacroix and Justice Thackeray are fictional characters to aid in describing Krieghoff's work.

TWENTY

Representation by Population

Most Canadians learn about Representation by Population in either middle school or high school. It is usually taught under the catchy name "Rep by Pop," which lends it a snappy sort of air, like "Top of the Pops" or even "Pop Tarts." Most of us can remember the "Rep by Pop" part, but what does it really mean? Surely, it must be a good thing, democracy at its purest and all that sort of stuff, yes? Well, as you'll see, Canada's English over-lords withheld "Rep by Pop" as a way to shaft the French, and when they did finally advocate its adoption, their main objective was to (surprise, surprise) shaft the French. For instance, what would happen if French Canada and English Canada were competing on some kind of live TV show and the winner was determined by who received the most phone-in votes? It would be really frustrating if one or the other clearly got more votes but the scoreboard always registered a tie…

"Rep Goes Pop!"

A Special Episode of…

So You Think You Can Responsibly Govern Canada

HOST *(voice-over): This week on* So You Think You Can Responsibly Govern Canada, *a special*

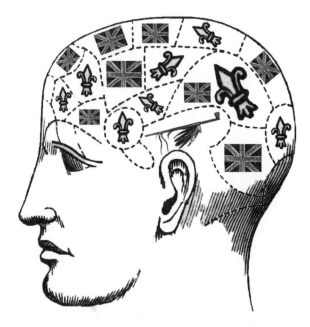

The national collective unconscious prior to Rep by Pop: by counting the number of Union Jacks and fleurs-de-lys, you can see how French and English concerns are locked in a stalemate because they have an equal number of votes. Often overlooked during this period are Aboriginal interests repressed in a small area of the subconscious just above the ear.

—⁓—

episode—"Rep Goes Pop!" Tonight, viewers from Upper and Lower Canada—also known as English Canada and French Canada—will call in and cast their votes on key issues of the day. But—and this is a big but—even though Lower Canada—that's Québec—has more people, there's no way it can ever outvote Upper Canada—that's Ontario. Why is that? Let's look back at previous episodes of So You Think You Can Responsibly Govern Canada.

☛ **Insert excerpt from Episode 105: "The Act of Union—1841"**

(The British Government sits behind its desk. In front of it, seated on two high stools are Upper Canada and Lower Canada.)

BRIT GOV: In view of both of your rebellions of the 1830s, Lord Durham's Report has recommended—

LOWER CAN: Well, that's great—we have rebellions—people die, and what do you do? Call a Royal Commission.

UPPER CAN: It's not a Royal Commission, it's a report.

LOWER CAN: If it looks like a duck, and it smells like a duck…

UPPER CAN: No, you're right. I agree, I'm just saying—

BRIT GOV: Lord Durham's Report recommends responsible colonial government.

LOWER CAN: That's great!

UPPER CAN: Yeah! Let's have a party!

LOWER CAN: Your place or mine?

BRIT GOV: But we're not going to do that.

LOWER CAN: Do what?

BRIT GOV: Have responsible colonial government.

UPPER & LOWER CAN: Oh…

HOST *(voice-over): Then the British Government drops a bombshell…well, as much as a bombshell as you can have in a reality show about 19th-century Canadian politics.*

BRIT GOV: We've decided that the two of you will be conjoined in…the Act of Union!

(Upper and Lower Canada look at each other uncertainly.)

UPPER CAN: Will it bother you if I eat crackers in bed?

LOWER CAN: No, but I snore.

UPPER CAN: You know, I'm not even sure I have those kinds of feelings for you.

LOWER CAN: You're right, I mean, you're Protestant and I'm Catholic.

UPPER CAN: You're French and I'm English.

(Upper and Lower Canada start to sing.)

UPPER & LOWER CAN: "Let's call the whole thing off…"

☛ INSERT EXCERPT FROM EPISODE 106: "TIL DEBT DO US PART"

HOST *(voice-over): After the painful break-up, the British Government tells Upper and Lower Canada that they have to live in the same house for the sake of the kids.*

BRIT GOV: You'll be sharing a House of Assembly—

LOWER CAN: Will there be cameras?

UPPER CAN: You always act up when there are cameras around.

LOWER CAN: I do not!

BRIT GOV: You'll be sharing a single House of Assembly, but—and this is a big but—

LOWER CAN: *You've* got a big butt.

(Upper Canada laughs.)

UPPER CAN: Shhh—you're going to get us kicked off.

BRIT GOV: This is a big but, BUT—even though French Upper Canada has more people, we English lawmakers have decreed that both Upper and Lower Canada will have an equal number of votes.

LOWER CAN: That sucks! This is not an equal relationship!

BRIT GOV: Oh, and Lower Canada, you know how your debt is only £95,000, and Upper Canada's is 10 times more at £1.2 *million?*

LOWER CAN: You owe £1.2 *million!*

UPPER CAN: I had those student loans.

LOWER CAN: Well, excuse my French, but that's *un phoc* of a lot studying!

UPPER CAN: What do seals have to do with this?

BRIT GOV: Anyway, we're going to roll all your debt together, so Lower Canada, you'll be paying off almost half of Upper Canada's debt.

UPPER CAN: Best prenup ever!

LOWER CAN: This sucks.

BRIT GOV: You also both have to change your names. Upper Canada, you'll be Canada West, and Lower Canada, you'll be Canada East.

☛ Insert excerpt from Episode 107: "Years Go By"

HOST *(voice-over): Years later, Canada East and Canada West unburden themselves on their video diaries with shocking revelations.*

(Canada East sits alone in the House of Assembly and talks to the camera.)

CAN EAST: You know, it's not so bad—now that some time has gone by, I don't think this is such a bad arrangement, because now Canada West actually has more people than me, and we still get the same number of votes—paying off Upper Canada's debt was the best £600,000 I ever spent!

(Canada West sits alone in the House of Assembly and talks to the camera.)

CAN WEST: Canada East thinks everything is great, but little do they know that Representation by Population is now a hot-button issue in this province. I mean, it was all very well to have an equal number of votes when it was to my advantage, but now that it's not, I feel differently, and I don't think I'm being treated fairly.

HOST *(voice-over): And now, tonight's special edition of* So You Think You Can Responsibly Govern Canada—*"Rep Goes Pop!"*

(Opening Titles Roll)

(Music and Applause)

(Host walks onto the stage.)

HOST: *Well, it's time to count the votes. The question is—should Canada East and Canada West have representation based on population? We already know it's a tie, because even though Canada West now has more people, Canada East gets an equal number of votes, and so that's our exciting conclusion—another year or two of governmental deadlock. But wait a minute, folks, because, we have some very special contestants tonight—Mr. John A. Macdonald and George-Etienne Cartier, Joint Premiers of the Province of Canada.*

(Applause)

HOST: *And that crowd behind them are the other people who helped make this possible tonight. Gentlemen.*

MACDONALD: Thanks, thank you very much.

CARTIER: *Merci.*

MACDONALD: Ladies, gentlemen and, of course—honoured judges...

CARTIER: Mesdames, messieurs et juges honorables...

MACDONALD: We propose a Confederation of all the provinces with the new federal government assuming all provincial debt. Matters of culture and day-to-day decisions will be at the power of the provinces and not the federal government.

CARTIER: *Nous proposons une Confédération de toutes les provinces avec le gouvernement fédéral assumant toute dette provinciale. Les affaires de la culture et des choix de la vie quotidienne seront à la pouvoir des provinces et non le gouvernement fédéral.*

CAN EAST: OK, well, I guess that's not so bad, because we are, after all, a distinct society.

CAN WEST: This is great—we can now squash you Frenchies like a bag of croissants, and as Canada grows, this will also mean that urban areas can outvote rural ones—good times!

HOST: *And that's it until our next episode. Until then, I want you to think of three words that are synonymous with good times: "Party in Charlottetown."*

WHAT'S REAL

Along with the personification of French and English Canada, all of the cheesy 21st-century metaphors give a reasonable sense of the antagonistic relationship between these two entities. The intents and outcomes, while ridiculously simplified, are basically accurate. One important difference—Upper Canada was not in debt because of student loans, but because of a series of bad investments intended to build shipping canals to service Montréal.

TWENTY-ONE

Cutting Canada's Border

Today, the border between Canada and the U.S. is, for most people, a line on a map and a serious inconvenience when trying to cross over because of tiresome security checks. But imagine cutting the border through hundreds or even thousands of miles of Canada's dense forests. That is precisely what a hardy breed of loggers had to do starting sometime around 1860. One has to assume that some of the men doing this rugged work would prefer to be remembered as nation builders, instead of toiling in anonymity—and what better way to get a bit of recognition than by being the squeaky wheel on the cart and writing a demanding letter?

The Bob McKutcheon Line

```
August 18, 1861
TO: John A. Macdonald and George-Etienne
Cartier, Joint Premiers of the Province
of Canada


RE: Please name the International
Boundary after me
```

Please read my letter to find out why I am sending you this
photograph. ~ BM

Dear Messrs. Macdonald and Cartier:
    My name is Bob McKutcheon, and I am
one of the lumberjacks who is cutting
a line along the 49th Parallel to mark
the border between the United States
and the Canadas. I am a simple man, but
a very large one. I am sending you the
enclosed picture to show you what hard

work it is. I am the blurry figure in
the foreground with my hands on my belt
buckle. Sorry that I am blurry, but I had
just inhaled some snuff and unfortu-
nately sneezed just as the photographer
was taking the picture.

I am writing to you because I have
just learned that the border between our
two countries is to be called the "International Boundary," and instead, I would
like you to name it after me—either "The
Bob McKutcheon Parallel" or "The Bob
McKutcheon Line." My reasoning for this
is that I am the one doing all the work
of cutting it out, and so it ought to be
named after me. Of course, I am not alone
in this work—there are plenty of us at
it, and I would be willing to settle for
some kind of name that would share the
glory, such as, perhaps, "The Lumberjack
Limit" or even "The Loggers' Run" or
something to that effect.

Mr. Gregory, the surveyor, has told me
about all the trouble the U.S. and the
Canadas have been having in figuring out
where the border should be. He told me
about the Aroostook War 20 years ago,
which is why we have the border between
Maine and New Brunswick and Québec. Mr.
Gregory says it wasn't a war at all but

that both sides had mustered troops and were ready to fight before cooler heads prevailed. Then he told me about the Oregon Question and how the Americans wanted to have all the land up to Alaska because the southern tip of Alaska is at the 54th parallel—that's why the Americans were all running around saying "54-40 or fight!" (I had always wondered what that was supposed to mean, and now I know—Mr. Gregory tells me that the "40" is the number of "minutes" that measures the east/west position of a place.) A few of the other lumberjacks and I have put a little camp band together (I play a very respectable squeeze-box), and we have decided to call ourselves "54-40."

Speaking of all these numbers and so forth, you may be thinking of simply calling the border the "The 49th Parallel," but in my opinion, the number 49 has not really done very much work and therefore does not deserve the honour of having a border named after it. Mr. Gregory also reminded me of what they called the "Pig War" a couple of years ago in 1859 out on the west coast when that American shot that Irishman's pig who worked for the Hudson's Bay Company (the Irishman,

☞

not the pig). I think the American's offer to pay $10 for the pig was perfectly reasonable, and it's too bad that the HBC man was such a duffer about it. But still, it's why we have a proper border out there now and part of the reason we're cutting out the border. So I guess by that reasoning, we could call it the "Pig Perimeter" or something like that, seeing as how the pig was the only casualty of the war. As with the number 49, though, the pig did not really do much except accidentally get shot and die, which seems like precious little enough to me, compared to cutting down hundreds—no thousands—of trees.

It's one thing to draw a line on a map—it's quite another to actually cut down thousands and thousands of miles of trees. I am kind of surprised that we actually need to do this, but I suppose that if we do not, there will always be confusions like the Pig War and Aroostook War and the Oregon Question. The thing that gets me, though, is that once we've cut the thing out, who's going to pay attention to it? It's not as though you can put guards every 50 feet, and besides, why would you need to? Just have a look at the picture I've sent—we're the

only ones out here. If you cut a border
through the forest, does anybody know
it's there? I scarcely think the birds
and the bears are going to pay any
attention to it. However, I *digest*
(I've heard Mr. Gregory say that).

Those are all the reasons I can
think of why you should name the border between the Canadas and the United
States either the "Bob McKutcheon Trail"
or "Loggers' Limit" or something along
the lines that I have suggested. And
if you could do that before November 9,
that would be wonderful; my mother's
birthday is that day, and I think she
would be proud of me.

Sincerely,
Bob McKutcheon

WHAT'S REAL

The photograph shows men cutting the 49th parallel in 1860. None of the men have been identified, and the characters of Bob McKutcheon and Mr. Gregory are completely fictitious. All of the various border disputes described did take place. "54-40" is also the name of a popular Canadian rock band whose heyday was in the 1990s.

TWENTY-TWO

The Cariboo Gold Rush

The Cariboo Gold Rush began in 1861 and brought eager prospectors to the Interior of British Columbia. Like other gold rushes of the mid- to late 1800s, the Cariboo represented the opportunism of the times; similar to the dot-com bubble of the 1990s, almost everyone saw an opportunity to acquire transformative riches—fortunes so vast that their very lives would be changed forever. In reality of course, only a few people discovered staggering success, while more than a few made a handsome living, and plenty of people probably made more money than they could have hoped to in any other profession that required physical stamina and native intelligence, but little in the way of formal education. Like any other relatively new endeavour, gold rushes also tend to bring out ideas that might have been big if only they hadn't failed so spectacularly.

THE CAMELS ARE COMING!

(headline from the *Victoria Colonist,* March 1862)

January 6, 1863 ~ Victoria, BC

FROM: John Calbreath
Merchant and Transport Entrepreneur

This Bactrian (two-humped) camel shows us the smug, loose-lipped grin that leads Mr. Calbreath to believe it is having some kind of joke at his expense. Perhaps he might have had more luck with dromedaries (camels with one hump).

TO: Frank Laumeister
Fraudulent Purveyor of Faulty Ungulates

  In March of last year I purchased
from you some 23 Bactrian camels at the
price of $300 a head. Your advertisement
of March 1, 1862, in the *Victoria
Colonist*, followed by your assurances
in person, led me to believe that the

☞

animals you were offering for sale had served with distinction in the US Army Camel Corps but had recently fallen into disuse. You informed me that you had in fact served with the camels as a former member of their Corps and that they would be ideally suited to the hauling of goods to gold-mining settlements along such routes as the Cariboo Road.

I am writing to tell you, sir, that your suppositions in this matter are not merely baseless and without foundation, but are, in fact, egregiously inaccurate. The camels you sold me are bad-tempered, obstinate and prone to spit. In spite of the fact that they can carry between 500 and 600 pounds (far more than a mule), I was disappointed to discover that the soft pads of their feet are vulnerable to the sharp rocks we have in these parts: we have been compelled to tailor canvas boots for them, which now adds embarrassment to my many other travails when passersby and even small children call out, "Nice Booties!" While camels may be suited to carrying loads throughout the sandy American southwest, I hasten to inform you that they are utterly unsuited to the more rugged terrain we have here in Canada.

☞

Their mulish temperament also leaves
much to be desired, and you can only
imagine my alarm when I learned that the
Camel Corps in which both yourself and
your camels served proved untenable, not
because of any physical defect on the
part of the camels, but rather, due to
their wilful and generally intractable
natures. To begin with, their large,
loose lower lips give me the feeling that
they are grinning knowingly at my expense
and, knowing what I know now, I suspect
they are. Second, you did not inform me
of their propensity for spitting; know-
it-alls and so-called experts have
informed me that the camels are actually
regurgitating contents from their multi-
chambered stomachs and "spraying" them
because they are irritated—as if this is
somehow less revolting than "spitting."
What I can tell you is that after I separated two camels that seemed to be
having some kind of altercation, I was
struck with considerable force on the
back of my neck by a wet projectile
even though I was several feet away
from either of the perpetrators.

You also failed to mention the camels'
tendency to swallow whatever might be
nearby, and in this area I can honestly

☞

say that I have owned goats that were less omnivorous. I'm not sure if you have noticed (what with being an American and all), but we are having a bit of a gold rush in these parts, and many dollars are to be made hauling over-priced goods into the wilderness and selling them to prospectors. I wish then that you would have informed me of the camels' indiscriminate palates—they seem to enjoy eating all manner of cloth, dry goods and even soap (which, surprisingly, does nothing to improve their breath). They have literally eaten my profits.

You also could have mentioned that horses are frightened of them. If the coach drivers here are not laughing at my canvas-shod charges, then they are fighting to regain control of their own terrified equines. We have a travelling judge in these parts—Justice Matthew Baillie Begbie—who travels either on foot or on horseback and hears cases from Victoria to Barkerville. He is quite a strict fellow, and obviously a judge is not someone on whose bad side I wish to be. Imagine my horror then, when I learned that somewhere on Cariboo Road, a team of your camels passed Judge Begbie, spooked his mount and caused the poor creature

☞

to charge off into the bush with the
judge holding on for dear life. They say
that Begbie cannot stand the sight of a
camel now, and I can scarcely blame him.

In closing, let me say that this gold
rush has been good to many—some claims
have yielded thousands of ounces of gold
and have showered their lucky propri-
etors with great profits—while I am but
a humble merchant. I had hoped to share
in these profits and hope yet to do so;
however, for the time being I must con-
cede that the camels I purchased from
you are in no way going to contribute
to my future prosperity. When we started
this venture, you had suggested that
I might serve as the representative for
you and your other stakeholders—I was
happy to do so when I thought that we
were proffering simple beasts of burden;
now that I know they are really spiteful,
double-humped demons, I cannot, in good
conscience, represent them to potential
customers as anything more.

I am writing then, to ask you for
a full refund for every camel I can
return to you in the state comparable
to that in which I received it. Shortly
after taking delivery, one of them gave
birth, and both baby and mother have

☞

disappeared to fend for themselves. Accordingly, I only have 22 camels to give back to you. I hope you will view my request fairly, as I feel that you have misrepresented the suitability of your camels to work in this climate. Also, because you yourself were in the US Camel Corps, I suspect you must have been well acquainted with their obstreperous characters.

Sincerely,
John Calbreath

PS: The locals hereabouts have taken to pronouncing my last name "Camel Breath," and I do not appreciate it.

WHAT'S REAL

Camels were introduced to BC by men named John Calbreath and Frank Laumeister in the manner described. It seems, however, that Calbreath was more closely affiliated with Laumeister than the fictional letter above suggests. Calbreath appears to have acted as a sort of agent for Laumeister and other camel speculators. Beyond that, all of the events referred to are alleged to have happened, including the incident with Judge Begbie's horse.

TWENTY-THREE

The Charlottetown Conference

In 1841, Lower Canada (Québec) and Upper Canada (Ontario) were amalgamated into the Province of Canada in a so-called Act of Union, and that was how it stayed for the next 26 years—there were as yet no western provinces, and the Maritime Provinces governed themselves. In September 1864, Charlottetown, PEI, was set to host a conference exploring the possibility of a union of the Maritime Provinces. It was attended by delegates from Nova Scotia, New Brunswick and, of course, PEI. At the last minute, a delegation of Canadians wrangled an invitation to attend as observers. There was also a circus in town…

Glossary of PEI Slang and Idioms

barkative: talkative

bucket under a bull: a foolish squandering of sound resources (for example, "as much use as a freezer to an Eskimo")

buggerlugs: a curmudgeonly oldster, likely backwards in his mode of thought

bumboat: a small boat often towed astern (rear) of a larger vessel

catawampus: askew, awry, out of order

coggly: shaky, unsteady or wobbly

cow's breakfast: a wide-brimmed straw hat that was supposedly the predominant head gear of rural folk

crow's piss: early in the morning

dilsy: a good-looking young woman

high dudgeon: a feeling of deep resentment

King Shit from Turd Island: someone seen to be arrogant

kittardy: a low-witted person

lorsh: an interjection combining "lord" and "gosh"

masheer: supposedly

not charmin' likely: not likely at all

rooms to let in the upper storey: describes someone not thought to be the sanest

skillick: a smidgen, often used in the negative: "He wasn't a skillick of help"

snollygoster: an unreliable or unethical person

sonsy: a buxom or jolly woman

strunt: to sulk, take offence or be in ill humour

throughother: descriptive of a house, room or situation in a state of confusion

tongues as oily as a churnful of butter: dishonest or misleading

Excerpts from

THE DIARY OF
HENRY CHAPEAU

☞ *Charlottetown's Only Purveyor of Gentlemen's Hats* ☜

Thursday, September 1, 1864

The nice thing about being a hatter is that even when people aren't buying a lot of hats, I still have time to stand on my stoop talking to neighbours. Of course I wouldn't count Coggly Pete as a neighbour exactly. He does, after all, sleep behind the outhouse at the post office, and he undoubtedly has rooms to let in the upper storey if you take my meaning. But he does have infrequent moments of undeniable lucidity, and if you can manage to converse with him during these times, some entertaining moments may be had. Today he was in high dudgeon about yesterday's arrival of the Slaymaker and Nichols' Circus.

"Lorsh, I never seen the town in such a catawampus," said Coggly Pete. "All the hotels are full with people coming from all over to see the circus. They have a troupe of acting dogs and some sort of comedian who's a monkey. And what about all the pretty ladies? Mademoiselle Elizabeth, *equestrienne non-pareil,* is said to be quite the sonsy. And they have some dilsy of a dancer called Miss Frank Nixon, though I never heard of a girl named Frank before."

Just then we noticed Mr. W.H. Pope hurrying up the street toward us. Mr. Pope is a very important person here in Charlottetown, being the provincial secretary. And yet for all that, he treats the rest of us respectfully and even tolerates Coggly Pete.

"Mr. Chapeau," said Mr. Pope as he approached, "quickly, please, I need to purchase a new hat."

"What has happened to that fine top hat I sold you last month if I may ask?"

"I attended the circus last night and a pack of thespian canines chewed the thing to bits."

"You saw the acting dogs?" Coggly Pete wanted to know. "Did they amaze and mystify?"

"No, sir," said Mr. Pope. "They chewed up my hat, and now I must purchase a new one."

We entered my shop and Coggly Pete followed. Had it been any gentleman other than Mr. Pope, I would have barred Pete from accompanying us, but as I knew Mr. Pope would not mind, I permitted it.

"If you don't mind my saying, sir, you seem to be in quite a rush," I said.

"Indeed I am, Mr. Chapeau. The observers from Canada are due to arrive today, and I must be properly attired to greet them."

"Observers?" asked Coggly Pete. "What observers?"

"Why the Canadian observers to the conference on the proposed union of the Maritime Provinces," said Mr. Pope as he scanned a shelf of top hats.

This was news to me, and I said so.

"That is because the entire town has ears and eyes for naught but the circus," said Mr. Pope. "Yesterday I couldn't even find hotel rooms for the delegates. And because the rest of my colleagues were off at the circus, there was no one to greet the arrival of the Nova Scotians, who took grave offence! Taking a lesson from our failure to greet the Nova Scotians, later in the day we accorded the New Brunswickers a most warm welcome and had horses and carriages on hand to transport them and their luggage to their accommodations. But I fear the press have only seized on this as evidence of a deliberate snub to the Nova Scotians, when really, I just happened to be away from my post for a moment as they arrived....How about that hat on the top shelf? May I try that one on?"

"Lorsh!" said Coggly Pete. "What do you need a bunch of delegates for anyway? Nothin' more than a bunch of barkative King Shits from Turd Island if you ask me. Boatload of snollygosters with tongues as oily as a churnful of butter. Unify the provinces? Not charmin' likely!"

"A majority of people on the island share your opinion," said Mr. Pope evenly. "However, we must

The Maritime delegates as imagined by Coggly Pete

discuss these things for our own good. Thank you, I'll take this one, Mr. Chapeau."

And with that, our provincial secretary paid for his new hat, sat it smartly on his head and strode purposefully down the street toward the docks.

Friday, September 2, 1864

Today I was standing on the front stoop talking about the circus with Coggly Pete when I saw Mr. Pope striding once more up the street, looking more than a little frustrated. I couldn't help but notice that once again, he didn't have a hat.

"Quickly, please, Mr. Chapeau, I shall require to purchase another hat."

"If you'll excuse my sayin', Mr. Pope," said Coggly Pete. "But if you're going through hats at such a speed, maybe you should think of switchin' to a cow's breakfast instead of these expensive toppers."

"Were I not engaged upon so much public service, I should not hesitate to adopt a more economical style of hat such as you suggest, but this week at least, I must appear in the attire of a gentleman. Now, Mr. Chapeau, perhaps this one on display on the counter..."

"Certainly, Mr. Pope, but if I may be so bold as to ask..."

"What happened to the hat I bought yesterday? Of course you may ask," said Mr. Pope. "Yesterday the Canadian observers arrived on their luxurious steamboat, the *Queen Victoria*. Not realizing that the *Queen Victoria* had its own lifeboats on board, as well as men to row them, I determined to go out on my own to meet the Canadians, which necessitated securing passage on whatever small vessel I could find on short notice down by the docks. To my dismay, the only means of transport I could find was a small fisherman's boat whose owner insisted on piloting her himself."

"A bumboat?" interjected Coggly Pete. "You rowed out to meet your fancy Canadians in a bumboat? You must have felt like a right kittardy."

"I did indeed, sir, indeed I did. All the more so for being seated upon an empty barrel of molasses amidships with a barrel of flour in the bow for ballast. And to my everlasting mortification, when the steward of the *Queen Victoria* saw us pull alongside, he mistook us for fishermen come to hawk our wares and called down, 'I say, skipper, what's the

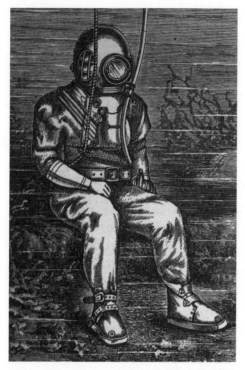

Provincial Secretary Pope takes a rest whilst searching for one of his many missing hats (courtesy Coggly Pete's imagination)

price of shellfish?' And as if these indignities were not enough, at precisely that moment a strong gust of wind blew my hat from off my head, committing it forever to the briny deep! I think I shall take this one and be on my way. Thank you for your time, Mr. Chapeau."

And with that, he was off again.

Coggly Pete and I went back to discussing the circus.

Monday, September 5, 1864

The circus has come and gone, and I never even got to see it. I would never dream of telling Mrs. Chapeau this, but how I wish I could have seen Mademoiselle Caroline *maitresse de chevale*—it all sounds excitingly horsey! On the business front, sales are booming because of the conference! Yesterday, as Coggly Pete and I stood bemoaning the departure of Slaymaker and Nichols, I saw Mr. Pope appear at the end of the street with four other gentlemen in tow, none of whom, I could not help but notice, had hats.

As they drew closer, I recognized none other than Mr. John A. Macdonald and Monsieur George-Etienne Cartier, Joint Premiers of the Province of Canada no less! I have seen their likenesses in the newspapers many times. Mr. Macdonald seems a jovial enough sort with a great woolly dome of curly hair that is going to grey. If he is as much of a tippler as they say, I could see no evidence of it, his eyes being clear and his manner alert. The corners of Monsieur Cartier's mouth are turned down, and the middles of his eyebrows are raised in an expression of focused intensity that may be somewhat imperious but does inspire a sort of natural confidence. The third gentleman was introduced to me as Mr. George Brown (of whom I have certainly read in the papers). He is the leader of True Grit Party, usually vocal opponents of the Macdonald/Cartier government, and I was surprised to learn that he was here. His face contains large, peaceful-looking eyes surmounting a robust pair of red sideburns—in truth there is more to his face, but beyond his remarkable eyes and luxuriant side-whiskers, I could not tell you what that is. The fourth member or this quartet was a stocky, solid man, the clench of whose jaw seemed to suggest bottled up power and the set of whose eyes made him seem eager for whatever he saw. He was intro-duced to me as Mr. Alexander Galt (of whom I have also read), no less a personage than the Minister of Finance for the Province of Canada! So these were the Canadian observers! And all stand-ing in front of my shop, apparently needing to pur-chase hats.

I ushered them in, and no sooner had we crossed the threshold than Mr. Pope grabbed me and Coggly Pete by an elbow apiece and hauled us off to the corner while the four Canadians examined the wares on display inside the front window.

"The most wonderful thing has happened!" Mr. Pope told us in hushed tones. "The four gentlemen you see now admiring your goods, Mr. Chapeau, have made an extraordinary proposal—a Confederation of the Province of Canada and all of the Maritime Provinces!"

"Lorsh! But that makes me strunt!" said Coggly Pete, turning to the Canadians with an unhinged glint in his eye. "Confederation! Why, there's not a skillick of sense in that! The whole thing would go throughother!"

"I take your meaning, sir," said Mr. Macdonald, stepping away from the window, "but we have presented our arguments in a most well-thought-out manner and answered all questions with unflinchingly honesty and ready wit."

"Mais oui," concurred Monsieur Cartier. *"Nous avons fait appel au cœur et l'esprit des autres délégués et jusqu'à date, nos propositions ont été bien reçues."*

Macdonald said, "What Monsieur Cartier is saying is, 'We have appealed to both the hearts and the minds of the other delegates and so far our proposals have been well received.'"

"This Confederation will be good for us masheer," retorted Coggly Pete. "But I'm willin' to bet it'll cost all of us Maritime Provinces more than we get out of it. 'Bout as useful as puttin' a bucket under a bull if you ask me."

I could see what Pete meant: conjoining our economic livelihood with that of the Province of Canada seemed to me roughly analogous to wearing a 10-dollar hat on a 10-cent head, the Maritimes being the hat and Canada the head, if you take my meaning.

"On the contrary, sir," said Mr. Galt, stepping forward with a suddenness that made the rest of us step back. "The new federal government would assume all debts of the Maritime Provinces, and the system of sharing income between the nation and the provinces will never cause a lick of friction so long as it shall last."

"But what about all those problems in the Boston States? This whole Civil War they're having is 'cause no one can decide whether the states or the government is in control!" said Coggly Pete.

Now Mr. Brown stepped forward and calmly said, "That is why we propose a system directly opposite to that of the U.S. In the Canadian system, anything that does not fall under the jurisdiction of a province is automatically a matter for the federal government to decide, instead of the other way around."

"Well, I may just be an old buggerlugs, but you have to get up at crow's piss to fool Coggly Pete, and there's somethin' about this that I just don't like."

And with that, Coggly Pete left.

"Well, gentlemen," I said hurriedly. "You appear to be in requirement of some hats!"

At this point, the four Canadians looked at me a little sheepishly, and Mr. Pope (who was holding his own hat rather protectively I thought) leapt to their rescue.

"Ah, well, you see, Mr. Chapeau, on Saturday, after Mr. Galt had finished presenting his arguments, the Canadians invited the rest of the delegates to lunch on their steamer, the *Queen Victoria*. It was quite an event I assure you, as it was the first

Delegates to the Charlottetown Conference and their hats. Sir John A. Macdonald is seated at the lower right (with his hat).

time that all of the delegates could meet in an informal atmosphere. I should hasten to add that the *Queen Victoria* has a supremely well-stocked wine cellar, and after more than a few toasts to the proposed Confederation, things became rather, well...convivial, for lack of a better term. It emerged that everyone felt quite warmly toward the idea of Confederation, at which point someone suggested it would be a fun idea to 'confederate' all of our hats into one giant hat, and out came a pair of pinking shears and some steak knives, and the rest I leave to your imagination. Suffice it to say, you will probably observe a steady trickle of bleary-eyed, bareheaded delegates through your shop this morning."

And with that, the four Canadians bought their hats and were on their way. And sure enough, as Mr. Pope had said, there was a steady stream of sheepish-looking delegates all buying new hats. Later in the day, I happened to walk past the provincial legislature and noticed the delegates standing on the front steps to have their photograph taken. I was proud to see so many of my hats proudly on display, held under arms and doffed to the midday sun.

Perhaps this so-called Confederation will be good for business after all...

WHAT'S REAL

The characters of Coggly Pete and Henry Chapeau are fictional. The PEI idioms used so freely by Coggly Pete are genuine, but in many cases would have been more likely to pop up in a rural setting, and some expressions probably did not appear until several years after 1864.

Slaymaker and Nichols' Circus was in town, but we are fairly certain that W.H. Pope did not attend. All of the equestriennes mentioned are listed by name on the surviving poster, as well as the troupe of acting dogs. Furthermore, all the visitors to see the circus did fill Charlottetown's 12 hotels. The Canadian observers did include the four men named, and their positions and roles as told to Coggly Pete are pretty much accurate, though the issues they argued were, of course, much more complex.

There is no evidence that either W.H. Pope or any of the delegates destroyed or lost their hats in the manners mentioned, though all of Pope's misadventures in greeting (or failing to greet) the delegates are true.

The luncheon onboard the Queen Victoria *was regarded as a special occasion since it was there that general goodwill toward the idea of Confederation seemed to crystallize into a united front. The* Queen Victoria *had a well-stocked wine cellar, and the luncheon was only one of many well-oiled social events held during the conference. On the last night of the conference, there was even a grand ball that went on until 4:00 AM. Contemporary observers wondered how much of a role good spirits played in the good spirits displayed.*

The Charlottetown Conference led to the Québec Conference later that year to hammer out the details of Confederation.

TWENTY-FOUR

July 1, 1867

Before it was called Canada Day, the July 1 holiday was known as Dominion Day. Since Confederation, it has been publicly celebrated across Canada. July 1 was proclaimed as a holiday with celebrations in cities and towns all across the land, and everyone knew that this was a historic day. But what was the very first Dominion Day like? From the 1860s onward, short stories called "School Stories" were gaining in popularity as suitable reading material for young men in the British Empire. During the peak of their popularity from the 1880s to the early 20th century, "School Stories" told wholesome tales about impossibly earnest lads from affluent backgrounds who went to private schools that were posh and Spartan all at once. What better place to set a story about the first Dominion Day than Canada's premier prep school, Upper Canada College, founded in 1829.

Dominion Day Escapades

JULY 1, 1867, WAS A CORKER of a day. The sky was blue, the breeze was warm and songbirds twittered in the trees. In fact, it was one of those days that seems to send its clarion call to all able-bodied boys on the verge of virile manhood. It was the sort of day that told them they ought to be larking through fields and so forth, engaging in all manner of wholesome pursuits perhaps involving campfires and swimming in cold lakes followed by plenty of vigorous towelling off. But there were no halcyon carefree pursuits such as these for the little group of senior boys now gathered on the front steps of Upper Canada College. Possessed of parents whose wealth was matched only by their indifference, the boys were spending an idle summer term at school instead of going on manly hiking vacations through British Columbia and all that sort of thing.

"I say, you rancid batch of indolent sardines," said Macdonald. "Let's venture on down to the lake and find a good spot for the fireworks."

"The fireworks aren't until 10 o'clock tonight, you giddy amphibian," retorted Brown. "And in case you haven't noticed, the current time is 10 o'clock in the morning."

"In any case, I'm predisposed to send some of the fags down to keep a spot for us," observed Mackenzie.

"Exactly," said George. "Why put ourselves out when there are perfectly good fags about to do the dirty work for us? The flatulent little simians need some sort of activity to keep their hands out of their pockets."

George's twin, Etienne, piped up, *"Qu'est ce que tu dit?"*

"By Jove, what a bunch of fug-loving layabouts you are," protested Macdonald. "I mean, dash it all, it's a public holiday to celebrate the coming into being of a new country—our country—Canada! And all you lot can do is laze about like pack of bilious anthropoid primates!"

The other boys cast sheepish looks upon each other. They were an unlikely group of friends. Macdonald's father was a crusading lawyer of some sort and was generally concerned more with the plight of the poor than with the schooling of his privileged only son. Brown's father was a lumber baron from Québec and, at this very moment, was presumably yelling at some lumberjacks 1000 miles away—even now Brown thought he could hear a faint, angry echo from the northeast. Mackenzie's father published a rather influential newspaper, but young Mackenzie could scarcely bother to remember what it was called. And finally, there were the twins, George and Etienne, sons of an east coast cod mogul. Their father was an uptight Englishman, and their mother was a boisterous Acadienne, which might help to explain the real tragedy of their tale, namely, that, through some misadventure of prior schooling, George only spoke English, and Etienne only spoke French.

"I do believe this queer old fungus is onto something," said Brown. "We ought to rouse our lazy bones and venture down to the lake. After all, a good set of fireworks is not to be missed."

"Indeed," chimed in Mackenzie. "There's no need for us to act like such utter swine that we can't stir our stumps for once."

"Well, done, Macdonald," said George. "You're not nearly the esophageal cancer you sometimes seem."

"Où est la plume de ma tante?" asked Etienne.

And so the boys roused themselves with much back-slapping and boisterous camaraderie. They were just about to set off down Simcoe Street on the first leg of their journey when "Black" Conrad appeared. "Black" Conrad was so-called because his family, through no fault of their own, were Irish (of the "Black" variety). He was a pompous, mean-spirited bully who was constantly bruising the buttocks of his fags with a cricket bat, just for fun. While the rest of the boys had gone to the All Hallow's Eve fancy dress party as pirates, knights and cowboys, Black Conrad had dressed up as Cardinal Richelieu, complete with white stockings that had the rest of the boys teasing him about his "lady-like" hose for the rest of the term. He had been caught selling answers to the Christmas exam but had somehow not been expelled. Black Conrad also liked to use large or difficult words in the hopes that no one else would understand them.

"What jejune pentad of comedo visaged juvenescence have we here?" said Conrad.

"If you mean to say we are a naïve group of five pimply-faced youths, why not just say so?" replied

Macdonald. "You're forever using big words and forgetting that we all take the same Latin class, you malodorous carbuncle."

"What vile perfidy!" Conrad ejaculated hotly.

"Oh, Conrad," said Brown, "I do wish you'd stop ejaculating all the time."

"I do not ejaculate!" ejaculated Conrad.

"Was that, or was that not, an ejaculation?" asked Mackenzie, turning to the other four lads for confirmation.

"Definitely an ejaculation," said George.

"Une émission nocturne, sans doute," said Etienne.

"What do you want here anyway, you unctuous boil?" Macdonald asked Conrad.

"I couldn't help but overhear your rather simple-minded plan to go down to the lake and view the festivities."

"He couldn't help but overhear, because he was eavesdropping," said Brown.

"Do you suppose he means our jejune under-taking to enview the pyrotechnic arts?" pondered Mackenzie.

"Enview isn't a word," said Conrad. "And I would remind you that my father's newspaper has a bigger circulation than your father's newspaper."

"That may be, but as far as I can tell, my father doesn't pay people to subscribe to his paper like yours does."

"That is an insignificancy!" ejaculated Conrad.

"*Insignifcancy* isn't a word," said George. "Now what is it you're wanting to tell us?"

"*Mon dieu!*" said Etienne.

"I consider you boys to be impecunious mentally if not financially, and so there is no doubt in my mind that you have heard of the plan to roast an ox at the foot of Jarvis Street tonight with the meat being fed to the poor," replied Conrad.

"I have heard something of the plan," said Macdonald. "And I note that you have just called us all dumb."

"Well, don't bother lining up for your slice of steaming ox," said Conrad. "For my plan is to slip the spit from its yoke, sending the ox into the ashes."

"*Mais pourquoi?*" said Etienne.

"Because the poor ought not have anything they have not earned for themselves," said Conrad. "That is a privilege only the rich should enjoy."

"As of today, this is the Dominion of Canada," spoke out Mackenzie outspokenly. "And all citizens have the right to universal ox meat."

"The Dominion of Canada!" ejaculated Conrad contemptuously. "I happen to know that our so-called prime minister wanted to call it the 'Kingdom of Canada,' but our good friends to the south—"

"I think he means the Americans," whispered Brown.

"…would not hear of such an outrageosity as to have a kingdom to the north of their border when their hard-won freedom from the yolk of imperialism is yet so recent."

"So let me get this straight," said Mackenzie. "You laud the Americans for quashing our English tendencies here in Canada?"

"I do."

"And yet you are obsessed with the trappings of English royalty. Don't forget that I sit beside you in trigonometry class, and I've often seen you doodling 'Sir Conrad the Great' in the angle of the hypotenuse—you want to get knighted."

Conrad went very red in the face and said, "We'll see how hard you're laughing when that roasted ox is ruined in ashes!"

Macdonald scrutinized Conrad and said, "Doesn't it seem unwise for you to be telling us this when we shall almost certainly try to stop you?"

The look on Conrad's face plainly showed that this thought had not occurred to him. "You are an insufferable lot of duffers!" he said before turning and bravely running away.

Our five intrepid heroes have no idea that history will ultimately regard them as a bunch of utter knobs.

⟶∽∿∽⟵

"I say," said Brown, "do you suppose he'll really try to do it?"

"Gangrenous appendage that he is, yes, I think he will," said Mackenzie.

"That sort of thing is simply not cricket," said George.

"*Oui,*" said Etienne.

"Well, then, chaps," said Macdonald. "It's up to us to stop him."

And with that the five boys ran down Simcoe Street with much hearty back-slapping and jingoistic waving of small paper Union Jacks the head master had given them.

"What do you think of all that rot he was talking about being a dominion and not a kingdom?" Brown wondered aloud as they jogged manfully along the street.

"Well," panted Macdonald, who was not so fit as the others, "he's right—we did rather hike up our skirts for the Americans on the issue of whether to be a kingdom or a dominion, but at least we got to be called Canada and not Northland or Anglia as others wanted."

"Or Victorialand or Albertsland," said Mackenzie, who wiped a drop of sweat from Macdonald's brow with his shirt cuff without breaking stride.

"Even worse would have been Borealia, Cabotia, Mesoplagia or Transatlantia," said George.

"Où 'Efisga,'" said Etienne. *"Un acronyme de* England, France, Ireland, Scotland, Germany *et* Aborigines. *En Français, c'est un acronyme de l'Angleterre, France, l'Irlande, Écosse, Allemagne et l'aborigènes—'Afieaa.' C'est un nom terrible."*

Although it ought not to have taken them any longer than an hour, what with all the manly jogging and Union Jack waving and wiping of sweat off each other's brows, it was inexplicably nearing dark by the time the boys completed the relatively short journey to the foot of Jarvis Street. Here they saw the gigantic ox carcass spinning slowly over a pit of red-hot coals.

"Well, that bounder Black Conrad hasn't gotten here yet anyway," said Macdonald. "That delicious-smelling bovine is turning yet upon its spit."

"That noble ungulate gave its life so that the poor may eat," said Brown, wiping a boyish tear from his eye.

"How on earth does he expect to tip the ox into the ashes?" wondered Mackenzie aloud.

"I see what you mean," said George. "The thing must weigh a ton at least."

"*En métrique, c'est 1.01 tonnes,*" said Etienne.

"Egads!" said Macdonald. "I see what he means to do. He's going to furtively tie a rope to one end of the spit and simply pull the thing over into the ashes!"

"How can you possibly know that, you erudite old wonk?" asked Brown.

"Because," said Mackenzie, "there he is, furtively tying his rope to one end of the spit!"

"Zounds!" said George.

"*Tabernacle!*" said Etienne.

"And look at that," said Macdonald. "The dirty rotten blackguard has bolstered his ranks with the fattest lawyers money can buy!" And indeed it was but the work of a moment to see that several corpulent lawyers were readying themselves at the other end of the rope to aid Conrad in pulling the ox into the fire.

"Never mind," said Mackenzie, producing a stout coil of hempen rope from nowhere in particular. "We'll show them." And with that he fastened the rope to the spit and flung the coil in the direction of his comrades. The boys began to pull with all of their nearly manly might, but the lawyers were very fat, and there were an awful lot of them. Conrad stood at the front of the line calling his opponents "oleaginous gobbets" and "ectopically displaced viscera," which had little enough effect since even if they had known what he was talking about, they would not have cared. The ox on the spit was moving slowly toward the lawyers and ashy ruin.

"We need more help!" cried Macdonald. "I say! All of you German, Irish and Aboriginal types waiting in line for your free ox meat—come and help us so that your compatriots may have their vittles—are we not Canadians?!" At this, a cheer went up and several ill-clad folk of bony proportions lent their skinny but willing arms to the worthy endeavour. But alas, the lawyers were fat, and the honest folk were thin—the ox shifted inexorably toward the ashes.

"It's not working," said Brown. "We need a stronger confederacy."

At this point, seeing the lie of the land, Etienne called out to a great crowd of Acadians and Québecers who happened to be loitering randomly in the vicinity, and with fearsome *joie de vivre* they lent their strength to the great undertaking. It was now that the tide began to turn, and seeing that the delicious ox would not be consigned to the ash heap, the Butcher of Ceremonies stepped up and began to carve. Never before had a slaughtered ox been butchered with such patriotic joy! The poor stepped up to receive their share of the steaming meat; the mouths of starveling babes were fed; the ravening bellies of their parents were sated; and wastrels just a mouthful away from their expiration dates were saved. Presently Conrad saw that his dastardly scheme would not carry the day, and gradually he paid off the lawyers who scurried back into the dark, damp crevices from whence they came.

Later that night as the boys reclined on the beach, linked arm-in-arm, Macdonald said, "You know, lads, we're dashed lucky to be alive at a time like this. How many people can say they were on the spot when a new country was born? Especially such a country as Canada!"

And with that, the first burst of fireworks sprayed up into the air. Ripples of hot red, white and blue light seared through the evening darkness, followed by explosive bangs, each one bigger than the last. But none of them were brighter than the glint in the eyes of the five friends, now conjoined by the bonds of nationhood.

WHAT'S REAL

In Victorian literature, when people say something suddenly and with much passion, they "ejaculate." You can find instances of this in everything from the Sherlock Holmes stories by Sir Arthur Conan Doyle to almost anything by either of the Brontë sisters.

In English private schools, "fags" were boys in their first year who were usually attached to older boys as servants and made to do all sorts of menial tasks. It is difficult to say how much the tradition of "fagging" was transplanted to the New World, but it's not hard to imagine that some of the spirit of the term made its way across the Atlantic.

The strange jargon the boys use and their vaguely Latin-sounding name-calling are quite true to the tone of real "School Stories."

All of the characters in the story are fictitious, though they are named after notable figures in Canada's

☞

political history and, in one instance, after a less savoury character of more modern origins.

In Toronto on the first Dominion Day, an ox was roasted at the foot of Jarvis Street for the poor, children were given little Union Jacks to wave, and there were fireworks.

All of the ridiculous alternate names for the new nation were actually proposed. Upper Canada College was also then located at the intersection of King and Simcoe streets and not at its current location just north of the city's downtown core.

TWENTY-FIVE

Louis Riel

Louis Riel—how does one write something light-hearted without actually making fun of this important but contentious figure in Canadian history? The solution is simple—just make fun of what people think of him today. And really, while we're at it, why not lampoon yet another phone-in show on CBC radio, namely Cross Country Checkup.

Cross Country Sound-off
(a call-in radio show)

"Rebel Edition: Who Was Louis Riel?"

LEX: Good afternoon. I'm your host, Lex Wordy, and this is *Cross Country Sound-off.* Today's topic is a contentious one—Who Was Louis Riel? To some he's a leader of two justified resistance movements who was unfairly executed for standing up for the rights of his downtrodden people. To others he's either a *delusional* religious zealot or a prophetic, *inspirational* religious zealot. For some people of Métis descent, he's a great leader who galvanized recognition of the Métis as a distinct cultural group. To other Métis, he's an interesting character, but his achievements are overrated. And so today we try to answer the unanswerable—who was Louis Riel? First the facts: Louis Riel was born in 1844 close to present-day Winnipeg. His family was part of the Métis community, a French-speaking people of combined First Nations and European ancestry. In 1869 there was widespread concern among the Métis that they would lose land they had lived on when the Hudson's Bay Company sold most of Manitoba to the newly formed nation of Canada. Louis Riel led a provisional government that practised armed resistance. Under Riel's leadership the provisional government also executed Thomas Scott, a political opponent accused of treason against the provisional government. The Métis' list of demands was eventually incorporated into the province-forming Manitoba act in 1870. In spite of being elected to parliament, Riel accepted a payment of $1000 from the government of John A. Macdonald to go into voluntary exile. From 1871 to 1885 Riel was in the U.S. and started a family as well as going into business and becoming involved in local politics. He also became increasingly absorbed by religious studies and intense prayer. By 1885 Riel was convinced that he was a prophet whose purpose was to lead his people against their foes. Back in what is now Saskatchewan, English, French and First Nations settlers were readying a long list of grievances against the federal government. Riel returned to Canada to lead them, but this time the rebellion was quashed, Riel was arrested, tried for treason and hanged in November 1885. Our first caller is John from Calgary. Hello, sir.

CALLER (JOHN): Hi, Lex. I just wanted to say that I think it's obvious that Louis Riel is the forefather of western alienation in this great land of ours. He led western settlers in a fight against the greedy federal government back in Ontario. I think if you do a bit of research, you'll discover that the slogan, "The West Wants In" actually originated with Louis Riel.

LEX: Well, that's very interesting, John. What evidence do you have that Riel said or wrote those words?

CALLER (JOHN): None whatsoever, but it's what I believe so it must be true—

LEX: OK, well, we have to move on now. Our next caller is Elizabeth from Manitoba. Elizabeth, hello. Who was Louis Riel?

CALLER (ELIZABETH): Hi, Lex. Well, I'm of Métis descent, and I see Louis Riel as an articulate, courageous leader who really cemented our identity as a people. I think he should be counted among the Fathers of Confederation.

LEX: I see. May I ask what your parents think of him?

CALLER (ELIZABETH): Well, they think he did some good things but that he was a raving lunatic—completely bonkers as my mum says.

And my dad calls him one of Canada's special losers, like William Lyon Mackenzie or Ed Broadbent.

LEX: What do your parents think of his decision to execute Thomas Scott?

CALLER (ELIZABETH): They think it was a bad idea, and so do I.

LEX: Alright, Elizabeth, thank you for your call. Our next caller identifies himself as a White Anglo-Saxon Protestant born sometime between 1930 and 1940. Good afternoon, White Male Protestant. Who was Louis Riel?

CALLER (WASP): Louis Riel was a bothersome thorn in the noble flank of Canadian nation building, Lex. When Canada was following the example of Great Britain and expanding its land holdings, that half-breed upstart Riel tried to put a stop to it and fracture our identity as a nation. Where does he get off doing that?

LEX: White Male Protestant, this couldn't have anything to do with the fact that you're a protestant and Riel was a Catholic, could it?

CALLER (WASP): I see what you're doing, Lex. You're trying to paint this as a case of English Protestants against French Catholics. Well, it won't work—Québec was just as much a part of Canada as Ontario, and it was the nation of Canada that Riel was fighting against.

LEX: So you don't think the settlers would have been treated any differently if it had been a French Canadian prime minister instead of a Scottish Presbyterian one—later an Anglican?

CALLER (WASP): I do not.

LEX: You are entitled to your views, sir. Next on the line we have François from Québec. François, who do you think Louis Riel was?

CALLER (FRANÇOIS): Well, it's obvious isn't it? He was a great statesman and a fighter for the rights of Francophones in Canada who were being oppressed by the Anglos.

LEX: But François, many of the settlers Riel represented were English speakers. In fact, his constituency, for lack of a better word, was made up of French, English and First Nations people, so how can you paint this as a battle of French Canada against English Canada?

CALLER (FRANÇOIS): Your factual point infuriates me, and so I choose to ignore it! Goodbye, Lex!

LEX: Next we have Steve, who's 14 years old and a self-professed comic nerd from Toronto. Steve, who was Louis Riel?

CALLER (STEVE): I just finished reading a graphic novel about Lewis Reel by Chester Brown.

LEX: First off, his name is pronounced "Loo-ee Ree-ell." And I've heard of that work and I believe it's a factual biography in comic form and not a graphic novel.

CALLER (STEVE): Whatever—it was really boring. I mean, why couldn't he be like other Canadian superheroes like Wolverine or Nelvana of the Northern Lights or even Captain Canuck? Why didn't he have any superpowers? I mean, he could have totally beat the North West Mounted Police if he could shoot flames out of his eyes or something.

LEX: You are aware that Louis Riel was a real person and not just a character in a comic, aren't you?

CALLER (STEVE): Why would anybody do a comic about someone who was real?

LEX: Moving on, we have time for one more caller—George Stone. Now you, sir, identify yourself as "An Historian Without Sources." What does that mean?

CALLER (GEORGE STONE): It means I'm too lazy to find sources for my opinions, but it also means I can say things that most people believe are true but that may be impossible to prove from a legal standpoint.

LEX: Like what?

CALLER (GEORGE STONE): Like, "O.J. did it," or "Ben Mulroney is the most annoying person on television, ever"—that sort of thing.

LEX: So who was Louis Riel?

CALLER (GEORGE STONE): I think he's become rehabilitated from being a figure scarcely mentioned in the history books to someone it's cool to support. In a more narrow sense, he's also become an inkblot for special interests in Canada—they see in him what they want to see. A lifelong Liberal would say he was a Liberal because he opposed a Conservative prime minister. The Conservatives would say he was a Conservative because he believed in God. Nudists count him among them because there are reports that when he was in the sanitarium in Montana, he'd run naked up and down the hallways, screaming, "I am a prophet!" Child advocacy groups point out that he was also a father but that both his children died quite young after he was hanged—would it have made a difference if their father had lived? Psychologists say he suffered from megalomania. Socialists say he wanted the workers to control the means of production. Terrorists say he used terror as a weapon in executing Thomas Scott. Sociologists say he symbolized the struggle of primitive cultures against so-called civilized ones, of rural against urban, east against west, French against English and Aboriginal against European.

LEX: Well, George, thanks for talking to us today. We may not ever be able to say for sure who Louis Riel was, but hopefully today we've come a little closer. Stay tuned next for the stupid gardening show that wastes the airwaves. If there's one thing I can state with confidence, it's that Louis Riel did

NOT die for stupid gardening shows on the radio, because if there's anything more boring than watching roses grow, it's listening to people talk about watching roses grow. I'm Lex Wordy.

WHAT'S REAL

The key facts of Louis Riel's life and struggle presented in Lex Wordy's preamble are accurate but grossly simplified. Readers looking for more detail should consult real works of history. However, all of the different opinions on what Riel represented have been put forth by various scholars and advocates at some point since he was hanged in 1885.

Finally, while I wish I could take credit for the wonderful phrase "one of Canada's special losers," I freely admit to lifting it wholesale out of Douglas Owrams's excellent article, "The Myth of Louis Riel" from Readings in Canadian History *(full publication information is listed at the back of this book).*

TWENTY-SIX

The Indian Act

The flippant tone of what follows may alarm some, but given the current attitude toward Aboriginal land claims and First Nations status, it seems entirely appropriate. The Indian Act of 1876 stemmed from the Constitution Act of 1867. More than 100 years later, we're still amending the original act. Go figure…

Professor Zeus Explains

The Indian Act of 1876

Indian Act?
Is that a fact?
Well, let's just see
What the facts may be.

By a white legislature
The "Act" was proclaimed,
But such nomenclature
Should leave us ashamed

Indians live in India, and the last time I checked,
We live in Canada—is that not correct?

Really, honestly, it ought to be,
The "Salish, Nishga, Ojibwe and Cree,
Iroquois, Mi'kmaq and Haida, you see,
Wyandot, Blackfoot, Innu and Métis
Odawa, Algonquin and Anishnabe,
Huron, Crow, Sioux and Sarcee
All the First Nations from sea to sea
Losing their land and identity" Act.

The Act itself was enacted by WASPs
Who buzzed and droned and tried to cut costs.
There were so many things they wanted to change
So many traditions to tie up in chains!

"Will you please get lost?"
Said all the First Nations.

"Not at all," said the WASPs.
"We made reservations."

Since long, long ago, before pennies and matches,
First Nations peoples were holding potlatches.
You went to the potlatch and gave if you could,
But if you were in need, you could take what you would.

And in the blink of an eye
The Act needed amending,
For the WASPs didn't like
All the giving and lending.

But the Indian Agents that Ottawa sent
Were quickly ignored, given up for Lent.
Frantic telegrams were tapped out in Morse—
The potlatch ban could not be enforced!

The same thing happened with sacred dances.
"We said if you danced them you'd be taking chances.
But you danced all the same without telling us where,
Or when, or how and—we didn't care."

So the WASPs amended more and more
From coast to coast, from shore to shore.

They banned, outlawed, proscribed and forbade,
And you shall judge what a difference it made.

All of this time, the Indians so-called
Were greatly alarmed and rightly appalled.
Their lands, their rights, their tribal nations
Were steadily poached by WASP legislation.

To claim their stake and stake their claims,
To stem the tide of WASP-ish games
Would take perseverance with plenty of thought.
And quite a few dollars more than a lot.

In nineteen-hundred-and-twenty seven
(Nineteen-thirty-eight, minus eleven),
Indians seeking money for court
Sought to raise funds for financial support.

So the WASPs decreed that to apply for funds,
Permission was needed from government bums
Who sat on their hands while giving the boot
To Indians seeking a share of the loot.

It worked for a while (decades, in fact)
But patience wins out and changes the Act.
A paragraph here, a subclause there
Slowly but surely, a breath of fresh air.

And in nineteen-hundred-and-seventy-three,
The Nishga nation in BC
Were fighting in court to restore their lands
To empower their people and strengthen their hands.

They lost the case, but the judges agreed
That long ago sans writs or deeds
The Nishga had title to the land they lived,
A title that once had been theirs to give.

Up until then the logic was lame,
That the Indians never truly had claim
To the lands they'd hunted, farmed and fished
And if this was the case, what was there to miss?

The WASPs had reasons and hair-splitting clauses
Why the Indians should give up on all of their causes:

"It's always been ours, but we're *letting* you use it.
Just try not to break, smash, lose or abuse it.
You're *usufructs* to whom we've loaned,
Free to use but not to own."

The Indians were gobsmacked, their chins on the floor.
They mustered their reason and waged verbal war:

"*Usufructs?* Is that even a word?
That's the stupidest thing we've ever heard."
Said the Indian bands, "By golly we'll sue.
Usufructs?...FRUCT YOU!"

While justice is scarce, and answers are few,
Consider the merits of this point of view:
First Nations people have set their own course,
Blazed their own trail and stewed their own stew.

Fur traders beat a path to their fires
To enlist their skills as trappers and buyers.
The commerce of pelts and the paths of trade
Were blazed by First Nations seldom afraid.

And what of the generals who knocked on their doors,
Seeking alliances and armies for wars?
Tecumseh chose Brock not for his flag
But because self-interest was in both of their bags.

We offer these verses, flippant though true
As a different way into the hullabaloo,
For treaties and claims are hard to relate
To peoples' lives and oppression's weight.

Tho' the rhyming scheme's loose, and the syntax is roomy,
Heaven forbid the prognosis be gloomy.
Tho' times are tough, and the struggle is slow,
Let's not lose sight of the will to grow.

If some do feel, say what you will,
That First Nations' claims are over the hill,
Rooted in the past and history's "what ifs,"
Do try to remember that what is, is.

Think not of victims or losses and gains,
Tread not in tracks that are always the same.
Look to the future, the path to the fore,
Lean to the wisdom that knows there is more.

Before things get worse,
Let us move fast.
These Nations were First—
They do not come last.

WHAT'S REAL

First Nations do have "usufructuary rights" to the land they live on. This means that they can occupy a piece of land, farm it, hunt on it and exercise all manner of other proprietary privileges, but they cannot actually own it. Beyond this, pretty much all that has been described in Professor Zeus' poem has happened, though it has not, perhaps, been expressed in exactly the words I have chosen.

TWENTY-SEVEN

Poutine on the Nile

In 1884, renowned British officer General Charles Gordon was besieged in Africa. He was sent to the city of Khartoum (in a region called "the Sudan") to evacuate the area prior to a hostile takeover by the religious leader known as the Mahdi. Gordon's old friend, Field Marshall Garnet Wolseley, was sent to rescue him. Wolseley had seen plenty of action in Canada and, among other things, was a key player in the suppression of Louis Riel's Red River Resistance 15 years earlier.

In 1869, Wolseley had been impressed with the Iroquois and French Canadian boatmen who had paddled and portaged his expedition to Manitoba. Although the true voyageurs had already passed into history, "voyageurs" was a convenient name for these skilled oarsmen, so that was what Wolseley called them.

In 1884, contemplating a perilous journey up the Nile, Wolseley asked for a contingent of 400 Canadian voyageurs to transport his expeditionary force of 4000 soldiers and their supplies. What follows shows how yet another piece of Canada's history may have been mislaid in someone's closet somewhere.

1 October 2009

FROM: Louisa Chronicler, Sub-archivist
Canada Archives

TO: Patricia Dantic, Head Archivist
Canada Archives

Hi Patricia,

We recently received a very old photograph album from the descendants of
one of the Canadians who accompanied
Field Marshall Wolseley on his expedition up the Nile to relieve General
Gordon. The problem is that all of the
photos have fallen out, and we have
only the handwritten captions to the
photos that were once there. (Well,
there are also a whole bunch of those
little corner holders that people used
to glue into albums to hold the photos
in place, but those don't really tell
much of a story.)

The captions are quite descriptive,
and I want to know if you thought we
should actually include them as part
of our collection. I've included notes
where things might be unclear.

Louisa

CAPTION 1: Newspaper clipping asking for Canadian volunteers, with headline "IMPORTANT TO BOATMEN"

Archivist's Note: The boatmen were Canadian citizens hired by the British government. In a masterful episode of fence sitting, John A. Macdonald unofficially cleared channels for the British to assemble their voyageurs, while not actually committing Canadian personnel. Macdonald wanted to avoid being seen to officially support the venture, but he also did not want to stand in its way. Those who signed up were paid $40 dollars per month plus a food and clothing allotment.

CAPTION 2: Boatmen's Revels—Members of the force pose for a photo during spirited celebrations in an Ottawa public house prior to their departure. Can you spot the man with the chamber pot on his head?

Archivist's Note: It's really too bad that we don't have this photo. The only other photo of the voyageurs in Ottawa are very staid ones where they're either posed in small groups or all standing in front of the Parliament Buildings. We know that the general public's patriotic fervour was running high, and the voyageurs even paraded down Wellington Street to the CPR station where a banquet had been prepared for them before the train journey to Montréal. But so far, very little information about individual private celebrations has come to light. I confess I'd like to see the guy with the chamber pot on his head!

CAPTION 3: Pretending to be blind men on board the Khedive's yacht *Ferooz*

Archivist's Note: Exactly what might have been happening in this photo is unclear. The Khedive was the Egyptian leader the British were supporting, and we know that for the first week or two, he carried the voyageurs up the Nile, towing their smaller boats behind his yacht. As for the "Pretending to be blind men" part, one possibility leaps to mind—we know that a Montréal optometrist presented each member of the force with blue-tinted spectacles (sunglasses) to guard their eyes against the bright Egyptian sun. Perhaps they were clowning around with the glasses, pretending to be blind? Not sure when the stereotype of blind people wearing dark glasses first came to be—maybe this is it!

CAPTION 4: Voyageur meets modern-day Cleopatra and purchases her loincloth

Archivist's Note: Again, I really wish we had this photo because I would like to see what's happening. Apparently the voyageurs were very interested in all the things they saw along the shores of the Nile (ruins and so forth), but what really drew their attention were the people, mainly the nearly naked women who went about their daily chores dressed only in loincloths. Although the voyageurs appear to have found this scandalously indecent, there is no evidence that they were anything other than fascinated by it. This photo would almost certainly show Captain Charles Denison who is known to have purchased a loincloth from one of the women for 25 cents, after which its former owner apparently scampered off in a sudden fit of modesty. The real question is how a Victorian photographer could possibly have portrayed this scene with fitting decorum? Even the casual, light-hearted tone of the caption is surprising. The event may have been restaged in pantomime with another voyageur standing in for the woman.

CAPTION 5: Voyageurs assemble their boats; boatman loses temper at rudder that doesn't fit, feigns smashing it over comrade's head

Archivist's Note: It seems fairly clear what was probably happening here. The 40 small boats (whalers) the voyageurs travelled in were specially built for the voyage at different shipyards in England. Aside from the hull, the masts, rigging and the tackle, 27 different pieces had to be assembled once the expedition reached Egypt. However, it quickly became clear that, far from being uniformly built, the rudder assemblies were custom fits—that meant that each boat had to have the specific rudder that had been built for it. And, of course, the rudders and boats got separated during shipping, so the frustrated voyageurs had to walk around and discover which rudder fit which boat. Since impromptu photography was nearly impossible because of the long exposure times, it seems almost certain that this particular gag would have been staged with all the participants holding absolutely still for a clear exposure.

CAPTION 6: Canadian skippers, British troops, sailing up the Nile

Archivist's Note: Hmm—probably this was not such an exciting photo—the boats could be adapted either for sailing or rowing. For the most part, the voyageurs were divided so that one or two were in a given boat with the rest of the "crew" being made up of the soldiers they were transporting. According to contemporary accounts, the voyageurs were reasonably impressed with how quickly the soldiers picked up the business of paddling and rowing.

CAPTION 7: Long exposure of fast water; ghostly figures "track" their boat through rapids

Archivist's Note: When the voyageurs came upon a set of rapids where the water was moving too fast to safely paddle a boat through, they divided up the men and stood on either shore holding ropes (called "tracking" lines) attached to the canoe that was still afloat—in this way they could safely guide the canoe through the rapids without smashing it on the rocks. The original voyageurs used this technique 100 years earlier, and canoeists still use this method today. But this was tense, tricky work, and the men on Wolseley's expedition couldn't exactly stay still while the photographer took the picture; the "ghostly figures" were probably the result of men moving around during the long exposure.

CAPTION 8: Celebrating Christmas with unwilling Bactrian companions disguised as caribou

Archivist's Note: By Christmas Day, 1884, things were getting tense. A note from General Gordon, smuggled out of Khartoum, informed the expedition that he thought he could hold out until the 15th of December before either running out of supplies or being overrun by the Mahdi's forces. And now it was the 25th of December, and the expedition was still at least a month from Khartoum. In spite of these worrying circumstances, our intrepid voyageurs nonetheless found time to celebrate Christmas. Apparently the British troops had even carried a plum pudding all the way from England for this very occasion! The caption of the photo seems straightforward but does offer some puzzling elements: the "Bactrian companions" would obviously have been camels, and the caribou disguise might suggest that the Canadians somehow attached fake antlers to the heads of the unfortunate animals. The puzzling thing is where they would have gotten camels to begin with. We know that at the beginning of the journey, camel riding was a popular novelty among the men, but by this time they were well into the heart of the desert, and any camels they encountered would have been wild—perhaps these were tame ones who had escaped from some passing Bedouins or other nomads.

CAPTION 9: Camp cataract: a tangled skein. Companions help to extricate one of their own from a web of his own devising

Archivist's Note: I have to admit that all I can really do is conjecture about this one. The expedition was so large that it might take a few days to pass a particular set of rapids. Someone realized (probably one of the voyageurs) that it was more efficient to station one set of voyageurs at a particular set of rapids so that they could become familiar with its particular hazards and could more easily track the troops' boats safely through the cataracts. Up till then, whenever the procession reached rapids, each boatload of men would have gotten out to guide their boat through—this meant that different teams had to negotiate the same rapids, each one making the same mistakes as the last. By encamping groups dedicated to one specific location, the journey went quite a bit faster. There would have been time for fooling around between the arrival of boats, and this photo might be of a voyageur having whimsically tangled himself up in a spare coil of rope as his comrades look on.

CAPTION 10: Is that a sphinx in your pocket, or are you just glad to see me?

Archivist's Note: This last caption was obviously written at a much later date—it is in ballpoint pen and modern handwriting. It may describe a photo from the homeward-bound leg of the journey. In January 1885, Wolseley realized that time was running out. The meandering course of the Nile meant that the route to Khartoum was anything but direct. If you imagine that the final loop in the Nile is like the curved part of the capital letter "D," Wolseley decided to send some of his troops overland along the straight part, thereby saving several days of travel time; his need for the voyagers had effectively ended by this time. Also, the voyageurs' contracts stated that they had to be back in Canada no later than March 9, 1885. Accordingly then, most of them were sent to Cairo to await passage home. Waiting to ship out, they enjoyed themselves greatly, buying souvenirs and seeing sites such as the sphinx and the pyramids.

Sadly for the English, Mahdist forces overran Khartoum on January 26, 1885, and beheaded Gordon; Wolseley's troops arrived two days later. But for the Canadians, it had been a great adventure in a strange land.

WHAT'S REAL

None of the photos described appear to ever have existed, but many of the lighthearted moments described did indeed happen; the voyageurs were amazed and fascinated by the nearly naked state of the Egyptian women they saw, and Captain Charles Denison purchased the loincloth of a local; the force was towed behind the royal yacht as described; a Montréal ophthalmologist had provided pairs of blue-tinted sunglasses; the boats for the expeditionary force were built in different English shipyards, and their subsequent assembly in Egypt was plagued by non-standard construction; one officer brought a plum pudding all the way from England and finally, some of the Canadians stopped for sight-seeing once the voyage had ended.

TWENTY-EIGHT

When Laurier Met Diefenbaker

Prime Minister Wilfrid Laurier buys a newspaper from 14-year-old John Diefenbaker. Hilarity ensues (not really).

HERITAGE MCMOMENT #4

FROM: Richard Wanker
Broadcast Executive,
Historical TV Channel

TO: Mordant Wit
Freelance Writer

Hi again, Mordant,
   We're really excited about Heritage McMoment #4: "When Laurier Met Diefenbaker." It sounds just like a movie, doesn't it? I was also interested to discover that Laurier and Diefenbaker were prime ministers of Canada, but not both at the same time. I always figured

that Laurier was a teacher because
a school is named after him in my
neighbourhood.

I also didn't know that Laurier
was that guy on the five-dollar bill,
but I do remember getting a five in
change once, and someone had drawn
all over him so that he looked like
Mr. Spock from *Star Trek*—that was
cool—you learn so much interesting
stuff about Canadian history in this
job! As far as I know, Diefenbaker
isn't on any of our money.

I told my assistant the other day
that I thought Diefenbaker probably
made his fortune in the popcorn industry, because of that popcorn in a jar
called "Orville Diefenbaker." My assistant said I was thinking of "Orville
Redenbacher," but I'm sure that
Orville Redenbacher was actually
one of the Wright brothers.

Sincerely,
Richard (Dick) Wanker

Heritage McMoment #4: When Laurier Met Diefenbaker

Suggestions for visuals: I think we'd see some writing at the bottom of the screen that says, "Saskatoon, 1910." (You know, like how they used to have that writing at the bottom of the screen in *The X-Files*? And then we'd be at the train station. And we'd see Laurier getting off the train, maybe counting through a wad of five-dollar bills with his picture on them, and then a paperboy, who's young Diefenbaker, approaches.

YOUNG DIEFENBAKER

Extra! Extra! Read all about it! Buy a paper, Prime Minister?

LAURIER

Why certainly, young man. And tell me, how is the newspaper business going?

YOUNG DIEFENBAKER

It's going fine. Would you like to hear my ideas about Canada?

LAURIER

What an amusing young fellow you are. I hope that one day you grow up to be a great man.

WRITER'S NOTES

Dick, you've finally managed to write something that is actually more or less accurate—you must have stayed up late working on it.

But in this case, my question is—so what? Laurier and Diefenbaker are important Canadians, and this meeting between them is interesting, but it is also completely inconsequential and has no impact on Canadian history or culture. The only reason I could see for including it in this collection is that it's kinda neat. Is that really what you want the Heritage McMoments to be? Kinda neat?

☞

But wait, you have, after all, called them "McMoments," and so I think I have answered my own question. I suspect if you could offer a free plastic toy with them, you would.

YOUNG DIEFENBAKER

I can't waste any more time on you, Prime Minister. I must get about my work.

(Young Diefenbaker walks off into the crowd.)

You need to think of some way to show or tell the viewers that the newspaper boy is John Diefenbaker other than the narrator saying so at the end. Maybe Laurier asks him his name. Don't forget that the viewers at home can't see the script.

YOUNG DIEFENBAKER

Extra! Extra! Read all about it!

NARRATOR

On July 29, 1910, Prime Minister Wilfrid Laurier buys a newspaper from future Prime Minister John Diefenbaker. Two great Canadians cross paths in a truly historic moment.

As I said earlier, this isn't important from a historical standpoint. And it sounds as if you're about to say, "You got your Laurier in my Diefenbaker."
"Oh, yeah? Well, you've got your Diefenbaker in my Laurier!"
"Two great Canadians who go great together!"

FROM: Richard Wanker
Broadcast Executive,
Historical TV Channel

TO: Mordant Wit
Freelance Writer

Hi Mordant,

I'm so glad that you thought the script was accurate. That could be because I let my trusty assistant have a stab at writing it this time. I do think it's "kinda neat" as you put it.

I guess we have to agree to disagree about whether or not it's important to Canadian history. I mean, just think about what Canada would be like today if we didn't have this story—we wouldn't live in a land where people know that two of our prime ministers met each other, and one of them was even the guy on the five-dollar bill! I think this is a real "anything can happen out of the blue" moment that shows paperboys they can grow up to be prime minister one day.

I think your idea about offering a free plastic toy with each McMoment is wonderful—maybe we could do a Prime

☞

Ministers of Canada Action Figure series or something like that.

I also think it's OK just to have the narrator say it's Diefenbaker at the end, because it creates a sense of mystery.

Regarding your idea to say "You got your Laurier in my Diefenbaker"—I do believe there used to be a series of commercials for peanut butter cups that went something like this: "You got your chocolate in my peanut butter" and so on. Viewers might get confused and believe that Canada's prime ministers were made out of peanut butter or chocolate. (I don't think any were, were they?)

Looking forward to working on the next Heritage McMoment with you: "The Munsinger Affair."

Sincerely,
Richard (Dick) Wanker

WHAT'S REAL

Apparently this run-in did happen. Later the same day, Laurier described the incident to the press, though of course he had no idea of who the forthright young newsboy was, nor that he would one day grow up to be prime minister.

Troublingly, there seems to be no actual proof that the newsboy was Diefenbaker, but in spite of this, the meeting is cited as fact by otherwise reliable sources such as Collections Canada.

TWENTY-NINE

World War I

With all the veterans of World War I now deceased, it's easy for subsequent generations to forget that this was a new kind of war—total war—in which all of a country's resources were channelled into the war effort. For many of the young Canadians who enlisted, war was a game played with toy soldiers in bright uniforms that fought in polite formations and were put away in a box at bedtime. By the time the war ended in 1918, 50,000 Canadians had been killed. It is difficult to imagine how awful the war was going to be, but the following exchange of letters offers a fictional glimpse into the minds of two young lovers who had no idea what they were about to get into.

We'll be Home by Christmas

September 14, 1914 ~ Montréal

Mon Cher Bobby,

    I have not been able to sleep or eat since I received your letter—I do not think that volunteering to go to fight in this war (or any war) is a good idea, and I am so worried about you. This war

☞

is the child of England, France, Russia
and the other belligerents—why should
we Canadians, so far away and so different from our mother nations, be drawn
into such a terrible conflict? National
pride you say? Some sort of moral imper-
ative? What matter are national pride
and moral imperatives compared to the
sighs that pass through our lips when
you and I are alone together?

As you know, support for the war is
not so great here in Montréal. The feeling is that because Canada is a British
possession, the British ought to fight
their own battles. Why should French
Canadians give their lives for the
honour of the British? Why indeed?

As you know, my mother corresponds
with a good many people, and she writes
frequently to Mr. King (or should I say
Mackenzie King as everyone seems to
call him even though I understand that
"Mackenzie" is actually one of his
given names and not part of his family
name). As you know, Mackenzie King is
at present working for the Rockefellers
in the United States, but he is a pro-
lific correspondent and also claims to
commune with spirits from beyond the
grave. Mackenzie King has written to

mother that he has had terrifying dreams about the war. He sees a war unlike any other the world has known; in fact, he sees a war that will consume the entire globe. He sees men mired in ditches or trenches, dead and rotting, dying for a few yards of earth. He sees terrible weapons that spit fire and spray bullets like water out of a hose. He sees a poisonous mist drifting across the fields, suffocating those in its path and blinding even those who run from it. He sees heavily armoured engines of war crushing men in their tracks. And perhaps worst of all, he sees the war lasting for years and not months.

Oh, please, won't you reconsider your decision? I know that we live in different provinces, but today it feels as though we inhabit different worlds. It already feels as if we are so far apart—if you were to go to fight, we would be, literally, half the world apart. And I would be so worried about you that I do believe I would age a year for every day that you are gone. Please dearest, won't you reconsider?

Your loving fiancée,
Marie

September 21, 1914 ~ Toronto

My Dear Marie,

What a funny old worrywart you are!
I shall come out of this just fine—I'll
have a ripping uniform to show off once
I am back, and you will be proud for
me to squire you about in what is sure
to be a colourful array of ribbons and
medals. What could be more dashing than
going to war? Mr. King's dreams are
nothing more than that—just dreams. The
idea of soldiers sitting about in muddy
ditches is simply ludicrous. For wars to
be won, there must be progress—hills
must be taken, land must be gained and
so forth. Trust me when I tell you that
no commanders would ever allow their
troops to languish or lie fallow in such
a state of near permanent entrenchment
as you describe.

Regarding all the terrible inventions
Mr. King has seen in his dreams, well,
I think that either you—or he—has
been reading too much Jules Verne.
The armoured tank you described is
well known from Leonardo DaVinci's
sketches, but it is generally recognized as being utterly unworkable
(along with that ridiculous flying

machine that has a horizontal propeller
on its top!)—so please don't worry
about 400-year-old inventions that have
no hope of seeing the light of day.

On the topic of the poisonous fog and
the fountains of flame that King sees
in his clairvoyant haze—well, once again
I think he has been reading too much
fiction. It reminds me of the poison mist
and the heat rays used by the Martians
in Mr. Herbert George Wells' "War of the
Worlds." Now, I know that the Hun does
not play by the Queensbury rules—he is
not cricket, so to speak—but I can
scarcely imagine Fritz sinking so low
as the Martians! You are right, however,
about the guns that spray bullets "like
water out of a hose" as you so eloquently
put it, but have no fear! The new helmets
the army has issued us are made of solid
steel—imagine that! What ills could possibly befall me when this old noggin' of
mine is protected by a sturdy metal case?

Whether this is Canada's war to
fight or not—I say that it is. Look
at it this way—if Germany conquers
England, what will happen to English
possessions abroad? By "possessions"
I mean Canada, among others. Before
you know it, we'll have the Kaiser on

☞

our money, and we'll be learning to decline German verbs—I daresay that verbs will be the only things German we'll be allowed to decline! If it were to come to such a state as that, I think you would have little hesitation in thinking that Canada ought to offer resistance to the Hun, and to that I say, "Let us offer resistance now!"

Need I remind you that France is also in this thing along with England and the Russians? I also know that many brave Jean Baptistes have volunteered just as their Johnny Canuck brethren have. I fail to see why you would think that support for the war should be so much less in Montréal when it is your motherland that has just been invaded (and in fact valiantly defended by the English troops who stopped the Germans at Marne only last week).

Finally, I must point out that I think this war marks a great opportunity for our country to find its own footing in the world, for we shall fight together not as prairie boys shoulder to shoulder with city slickers or as English arm in arm with French, but as *Canadians*—and this if nothing else makes this venture a worthy one.

☞

Please don't worry, *ma cherie*—this war will never last, and I shall be home by Christmas, sitting by the fire and reading those dashed silly "School Stories" you so happily upbraid me for not having grown out of.

Your loving (and *living*),
Bob

"Modern" machine guns had been around since the end of the 19th century, but the major European powers had not used them extensively against one another until World War I.

Early automatic weapons offered the chance to fire and be fired upon in a highly uncomfortable sitting position.

WHAT'S REAL

With the exception of the machine gun, most of the innovations in weaponry described first saw use in World War I. They may have seen action before in a skirmish here or in an uprising quashed there, but their widespread use was largely unknown prior to 1914. The differences of opinion between French and English Canada as to whether Canada should join the war are well known, even though many enlisted from both groups. Future Prime Minister William Lyon Mackenzie King did work for the Rockefellers during the war, and despite his well-known predilection for séances in later life, I have invented the seemingly clairvoyant dream described in Marie's letter.

THIRTY

Prohibition, Income Tax and the Vote for Women

(OH, AND ALSO SOME SECRET UNDERGROUND TUNNELS)

Readers fearing the worst for Bobby (in the preceding letters about World War I) can read on with some relief.

He had survived The War to End All Wars, but could he survive coming home to a teetotalling, suffragist fiancée who constantly foisted earthenware jugs full of water on him when all he wanted was a gin and tonic so he could practise his repertoire of declamatory gestures?

September 24, 1919 ~ Toronto

Cher Bobby,
   Now that we are wife and husband,
I do hope that this separation will not
put too much of a strain on our young
marriage. We have discovered that we
disagree on many things: the Temperance
Movement, whether women should have the
vote, whether mental incompetents should
be sterilized, and so forth. I just hope
that the distance between Montréal and
Moose Jaw will not prove to be too much
for us.
   I am glad that you have a good job
with the CPR, but I just wish they could
have found some work for you closer to
home. I confess that at first I was
relieved you were leaving Québec because
of the recent repeal of our very sensi-
ble Prohibition Act—once more the gates
have opened for the wanton consumption
of intoxicating liquors. But now, even
though Saskatchewan is still "dry,"
I find myself worrying that you will be
led astray in your new home. I know how
you love to indulge in that vice which
so often earns my disapproval, and without your Marie close by to temper your

☞

thirst for the demon spirit, I fear you
may utterly succumb to its pernicious
influence. It is well known that
American gangsters drive up from the
U.S., bringing with them barrels of
the awful stuff to quench the throats
of Canadians too bereft of common
sense to see that Prohibition is good
for their health and their morals.
I have even heard rumours that these
purveyors of illegal drink have dug
tunnels under the streets of Moose Jaw
so as to escape capture.

Also, I know you cannot understand
why on earth a woman should want to
vote, but here again I know that the
prairies are a hotbed of progressive
views. Why, Nellie McClung herself lives
just next door to you in Alberta. The
great tide of universal suffrage that
has, this very year, swept across the
rest of Canada must soon come home to
La Belle Province, and I wait with bated
breath for that great day—surely it will
come soon! I wonder if your mere physical proximity to Mrs. McClung might sway
you closer to her view that the congeni-
tally insane ought not to be permitted to
reproduce. I remember that in a moment
of heated argument, you compared this

☞

practice to the castration of bulls, but really, human beings and bulls are very different creatures, and to suggest that we are treating them in similar fashion is both impolite and immoral.

Well, that is all I have time for today. I hope this letter finds you both well and abstemious, my sweet.

Temperately yours,
Marie

—∾∾∾—

October 1, 1919 ~ Moose Jaw

Dear Marie,

I have nothing against women having the vote, but I just don't understand whose idea it was to pair this issue with that of prohibition—it is well known that the Women's Christian Temperance Union and the Women's Suffrage Movement are, for all intents and purposes, the same thing. What baffles me is why anyone would think that denying a man a good stiff drink is anymore likely to make him vote for

☞

women to be enfranchised as voters.
If a man is just getting home from work
(or, for that matter, from fighting in
a war the likes of which the world has
never seen), he definitely needs a good
stiff drink, and it doesn't help matters
when his wife tells him that not only
has she poured all the liquor down the
loo but also that he will be sleeping
on the couch until he marches in the
voting rally with her.

I am the only man I know of who is
willing to march in support of women's
suffrage, but there is no way on God's
green earth I am doing it without a drink
inside me. Also, I realize that alcohol-
ism is a growing problem (especially
among men returning from the war) but
honestly, just because I have a drink
or two when I get home, do you truly
see me as some sort of addled, booze-
crazed addict?

I believed in many foolish things
before I enlisted, one of them being
the assumption that I would return
home with both of my legs. I saw
many horrible things during the war,
most of which I cannot get out of my
mind—they flash through my head even
as I sit in my nice, quiet office here

☞

in Moose Jaw. A drink or two when
I get home helps me to forget, and it
numbs the phantom pain where my right
foot used to be. I think I was also
foolish because I assumed that things
would never change, and now I see that
the war, among other things, has visited
great change upon this world, and much
of it is for the worse.

Having seen men slaughter each other
like cattle, you will have to forgive me
if I disagree with your Mrs. McClung's
unwavering support of the sterilization
of those deemed mentally unfit. I know
that it is stylish and "progressive"
to embrace this idea, but just because
something is widely accepted does not
make it right. As you know, I have never
found your father to be the brightest
apple in the basket, nor the most
socially apt—if he had been sterilized,
so that you would never have been born,
I would still be seeking a mate and
companion. That is certainly a very
sad idea to me.

As for Moose Jaw, it is quite a pleas-
ant city, and one reason I like it is
because I can see change in action—but
for the better. This little city is
bursting with vitality and energy!

☞

For instance, I think you imagine me languishing away in some sort of backwater on the prairies, but things are quite modern here I assure you. Why, Joyner's, one of the local department stores, even has a cash cable, just like Eaton's. You give the clerk your money, she puts it into a little box, attaches it to a cable and whoosh! Off it goes up to the accounting department where they audit the bill, make the change, put it in another little box and—whoosh—they send it back to your clerk all in the blink of an eye. I know you are familiar with this system, but I suppose I am describing it in such detail because I find it so soothing to watch the little silver boxes zooming all over the store as people make their purchases.

It is true that Saskatchewan is still "dry" as you put it, but I cannot see this lasting for much longer. As well as the American bootleggers, there is also a thriving local industry in "mash" here; that is, alcohol made by farmers in their barns. Why, only last week, a farmer dumped his entire batch into his creek to escape detection by the police. His cows happened to wander by a short while later, and, having drunk

☞

from the creek, the happy creatures were
seen leaning unsteadily against the fence
for the next couple of days—so you see,
if there are any drunkards hereabouts,
they are of the bovine variety.

The supposed tunnels you refer to
are nothing more than a ridiculous
myth—the gullible believe that they
are used for everything from hiding
illegal liquor to concealing Chinese who
are hiding from Head Tax inspectors.
While illegal liquor and perfectly legal
Chinese abound, I can assure you that
they are not hidden in tunnels.

A city ordinance here says that all
buildings with coal furnaces must pass
a fire inspection, and because the fire
inspection costs money, some businesses
knocked holes in their basement walls
so that the inspectors don't have to
go outside every time they finish an
inspection. And the inspectors, grate-
ful for not being exposed once more
to the elements, give these businesses
a cut-rate for the inspections.

I should also mention that Moose Jaw
is a friendly city (they will probably
put that on a sign at the city limits
one day), and during winter, I am told
the sociable merchants like to visit

☞

each other through the holes made for the inspectors. Perhaps these are the tunnels that people believe in.

It is also conceivable that the coal chutes here might be mistaken for tunnels—they are just like the coal chutes in Montréal and Toronto, having no other function more sinister than allowing colliers to dump a week's worth of coal from street level into the basement where the furnace is. But I can only imagine such a misconception springing up many years from now when people have forgotten what coal chutes are.

Well, this letter is already longer than I had intended it to be, and I had better be getting to bed soon. Please rest assured that I am just fine here and am exercising all due moderation. Hah! I think that we might each be happier in the other's location. There is prohibition in Saskatchewan but not in Québec, but there is also voting for women in Saskatchewan, but none in Québec. I know you hope that the tide of female suffrage will soon wash over the borders of your home province, but I wouldn't be surprised if you had to

☞

wait another 20 years or so for that
to happen—old habits die hard.

Your loving Bob

PS: I think I was also foolish to believe
that the so-called income tax, "temporarily" introduced two years ago to pay
down the war debt, would ever go away.
Not only have I lost a leg in the war,
now I have to pay for it too!

WHAT'S REAL

Most Canadian provinces repealed Prohibition one by one throughout the 1920s. Saskatchewan rolled it back in 1924—just in time to cash in on American Prohibition that lasted from 1920 until 1933. This meant that the flow of illegal liquor reversed: instead of Americans sending booze north into Canada, we sent it south to them. Québec had Prohibition for only a brief period in 1919 before it was repealed.

☞

The Temperance Movement was closely allied with voting rights for women, the feeling being that if drinking could be eliminated and women could vote, many of society's ills would vanish.

As for female suffrage, in Canada, women could vote in some provinces beginning in the late 1800s but only in municipal elections. National suffrage did not arrive until 1919 (except in Québec—the province did not allow women to vote until 1940). It is worth pointing out that Canadians of Asian heritage were not allowed to vote until 1947, and members of First Nations were not enfranchised until (wait for it)…1960! Is that any sort of civil rights record for us to be proud of?

The alleged tunnels under the streets of Moose Jaw are a well-known myth, and the different theories presented by Bob are in keeping with those who don't believe they ever existed.

Moose Jaw did have a thriving Chinese community, largely made up of the workers and families brought to Canada as cheap labour to build the CPR.

Income tax really was introduced as a "temporary" measure in 1917 to pay for the war.

THIRTY-ONE

Tommy Douglas
and Medicare

There are plenty of Canadians alive today who don't know that Kiefer Sutherland (star of the TV show 24) *is the grandson of Tommy Douglas, father of universal healthcare in Canada. What would happen if Kiefer were to star in a movie about his grandfather's life? And what if, unable to sustain a plot (though there's drama aplenty), the filmmakers, being Canadian, had simply thrown plot out the window (*32 Short Films about Glenn Gould, *I'm looking at you). Furthermore, and finally, what if they ran out of money part way through?*

24 Short Films about Tommy Douglas
(*starring* Kiefer Sutherland)

EXTERIOR. ROOFTOP. DAY.

TITLES: Winnipeg, Manitoba. June 21, 1919. Bloody Saturday

(Young Tommy and his Friend are two boys, both about 15 years old. They stand on a downtown rooftop and survey the chaos in the street below.)

EXTERIOR. STREET. DAY.

(Police on horseback surge against a crowd of Citizens all on foot. The Citizens are mainly men, a mixture of shabbily dressed as well as others who are somewhat more affluent without being posh. On one side of the street is an overturned burning streetcar. Citizen #1 runs by and trips in front of the burning streetcar. Cop #1 runs up and starts hitting Citizen #1 with a heavy wooden baton. Two or three gun shots ring out, off-screen.)

EXTERIOR. ROOFTOP. DAY.

(A bullet smashes into the chimney between Young Tommy and his Friend. They both duck behind the chimney.)

YOUNG TOMMY: This isn't a general strike; it's a civil war!

FRIEND: The workers just want a fair shake is all.

YOUNG TOMMY: When the powers that be can't get what they want, they're always prepared to resort to violence or any sort of hooliganism.

FRIEND: Hooliganism. Good word.

(Tommy seems to agree and smiles with a humorous glint in his eye.)

CUT TO:
INTERIOR. BOXING RING. NIGHT.

(A Roaring Crowd of about 1000 fills a hot, smoky boxing arena.)

BOXING RING—OPPONENT'S POV OF TOMMY

(Tommy has grown into a taut, wiry young man in boxing shorts and gloves. He bounces around his Opponent and throws punches and ducks blows by Opponent's fists, also in boxing gloves.)

TITLES: Winnipeg Manitoba, 1922

(Tommy lands some good punches, but the Opponent sneaks one in and Opponent's POV moves in for a closer view of Tommy standing woozily, stunned. The picture wobbles dreamily.)

TOMMY'S DREAM

INTERIOR. HOSPITAL WARD. DAY.

(A Young Boy of about 10 lies in a hospital bed. His Concerned Parents surround the bed. A white-coated Doctor confers with them.)

DOCTOR: Ordinarily in cases of osteomyelitis like this one, I'd recommend amputating young Tommy's leg.

TOMMY'S MOTHER: Oh dear.

DOCTOR: But as it happens, there's a risky new procedure I've been wanting to try out for some time. Of course, if you were to let me use Young Tommy as my human guinea pig, I would perform the operation for free. If it doesn't work, then we'll amputate his leg, which we'd have to do anyway. If it does work, then he'll still be able to use his leg.

TOMMY'S MOTHER: Free operation?

TOMMY'S FATHER: Where do we sign?

(The picture wobbles dreamily.)

INTERIOR. BOXING RING. NIGHT.

TOMMY'S OPPONENT POV

(The Roar of the Crowd is muted and watery. Tommy abruptly comes out of his reverie and focuses. He talks to himself.)

TOMMY: The only reason I'm in this ring today is because I had medical attention that didn't cost my family anything. Wouldn't it be something if everyone in Canada had free medical attention?

OPPONENT (male, off-screen): Hey, Douglas, you gonna fight or you gonna stand there all night spoutin' poetry and dramatic monologues and such?

(Tommy starts bouncing around his Opponent once more, punctuating his words with punches, a pugnacious glint in his eye.)

TOMMY: No, I'm gonna fight. I'm gonna fight for all the little kids with sprained ankles whose families can't afford doctors. I'm gonna fight for the regular folks trynna make a living. I'm gonna fight for the chumps like you who don't yet know that they need medical attention.

(Tommy lands a smashing blow to his Opponent; the Opponent's POV wobbles and finally falls. The Ref leans in, going in and out of focus. Ref administers the count.)

REF: 1…2…3…4…5…6…7…8…9…10.

(Ref stands up out of Opponent's POV.)

REF (off-screen): Ladies and gentlemen, the new Lightweight Boxing Champion of Manitoba, Tommy Douglas!

(The Roar of the Crowd fades out. Flickering Black-and-White Film Titles appear.)

SILENT FILM TITLES: Tommy becomes a popular local preacher.

(B&W Film shows Tommy preaching, shaking hands and signing autographs.)

SILENT FILM TITLES: In the autograph book of one follower he writes: "Instead of giving gems or flowers, we could drop a beautiful thought into the heart of a friend, that would be giving as the angels give."

(B&W Film shows Tommy handing the book back with a righteous glint in his eye.)

DISSOLVE TO:
INTERIOR. TOMMY'S STUDY. LATE AFTERNOON.

(Tommy sits behind his desk with a stern look on his face. Whinging in front of him are five Boy Ragamuffins, ages 10–14. Boy Ragamuffin #1 stands slightly forward of the others, wringing a shabby cloth cap in his hands.)

BOY RAGAMUFFIN #1: Honest, Mr. Douglas, we appreciate you takin' us in off the street, and we're

real sorry for stealin' those cigarettes and choco-
lates from the store after the fact.

TOMMY: I'm giving you another chance, boys,
but don't do it again. You can go now.

ALL BOY RAGAMUFFINS: Aw, thank you so
much, sir.

*(As a group, the Boy Ragamuffins shuffle backwards
casually to the door and smoothly make their way out.
Boy Ragamuffin #1 is the last one out, but he pokes his
head back round the corner.)*

BOY RAGAMUFFIN #1: Mr. Douglas?

*(Boy Ragamuffin #1 politely but deliberately re-enters the
room and approaches Tommy's desk. Tommy's face is
grave.)*

BOY RAGAMUFFIN #1: We're also real sorry for
stealin' all this stuff while we was in here just now.

*(One by one, Boy Ragamuffin #1 sets a handful of things
on Tommy's desk.)*

BOY RAGAMUFFIN #1: Here's yer watch what
we took, sir, and also yer fountain pen, as well as
yer penknife and probably this particular wallet is
one that you'll be looking for soon I dare say, sir.

*(Boy Ragamuffin #1 shuffles out again. Tommy looks
down at the items on his desk, up at the now empty doorway and back down at the things on his desk, a baffled
glint in his eye.)*

CUT TO:
INTERIOR. COUNTRY FARM HOUSE. DAY

TITLES: Weyburn, Saskatchewan. 1931

(Tommy stands at an old-fashioned wall-mounted phone with separate ear and mouthpiece. He listens but says nothing, becoming more agitated as the person on the other end continues speaking. Finally, Tommy breaks in forcefully and a bit testily.)

TOMMY: I'm proud to be organizing the unemployed in Weyburn, and if you want to call me a socialist for helping other people, then I stand guilty as charged. I believe that any society, most of all a Christian society, is measured by what it does for the aged, the sick, the orphans and the less fortunate who live in our midst...Yes, you can quote me on that!

(Tommy slams the earpiece down into its holder but misses, fumbles the spinning earpiece and gets tangled up in the cord. Finally, Tommy sorts out the situation and deliberately places the earpiece in its cradle, a frustrated glint in his eye.)

CUT TO:
INTERIOR. TOMMY'S OFFICE. DAY

TITLES: Weyburn, Saskatchewan. 1935

(Tommy sits at his desk listening on a slightly more up-to-date phone with a receiver and so forth. The Superintendent's voice is heard on the other end.)

SUPERINTENDENT: Tommy, me and rest of the superintendents of the Baptist churches in Saskatchewan really appreciate all the work you've done with the poor, and you do a lot of good with your preaching, too. But I'm calling to tell you that if you don't give up your political candidacy for this Canadian Communist League—

TOMMY: It's the Canadian Commonwealth Federation, Superintendent.

SUPERINTENDENT: If you run as a candidate for this CCF, then I personally will see to it that you never preach in this province again.

(Tommy speaks forcefully, a steely glint in his eye.)

TOMMY: You've just given the CCF a candidate.

CUT TO:
INTERIOR. SCHOOL HOUSE. NIGHT

TITLES: Odessa, Saskatchewan. 1935

(Tommy stands in the classroom in front of a blackboard with "CCF" written on it.)

TOMMY: Alright, and thank you for coming out tonight.

(A surly group of Young Miscreants charge the stage and surround Tommy. Tommy picks up a water jug and backs away from them, smashing the jug on the podium and holding the jagged weapon between himself and the oncomers.)

MALE VOICE (off-screen): Any trouble, Tommy?

WIDE VIEW

(A group of Young Men fill the doorway to the school house. The Miscreants look worried. Tommy has a flinty glint in his eye.)

TOMMY: Not now.

DISSOLVE TO:
INTERIOR. LEGION HALL. NIGHT.

(Men and women sit at tables along the walls of the hall, answering phones.)

TITLES: Provincial Election, 1944

(Tommy stands at one table with a phone receiver to his ear.)

TOMMY: That's great news! Great news! Hey, everybody, we won!

(Tommy slams down the receiver in good spirits, a triumphant glint in his eye. A Supporter rushes up and slaps him on the back.)

SUPPORTER: Congratulations—Premier Douglas!

DISSOLVE TO:
INTERIOR. SCHOOL HOUSE. NIGHT.

(The classroom is packed. Tommy stands at the front.)

TOMMY: As the premier of Saskatchewan, I promise you I'm doing everything I can to make things better for your kids, like making sure that all of the schools in this province have electricity.

(A Burly Man stands up at the back.)

BURLY MAN: Electricity to every school in the province? You'll never do it, Douglas. You're a dreamer.

(Tommy just looks at the Burly Man and smiles, a confident glint in his eye.)

DISSOLVE TO:
INTERIOR. TOMMY'S OFFICE. DAY.

(Tommy sits behind his desk, listening intently on the phone.)

TITLES: Saskatchewan Doctors' Strike. 1961

TOMMY: I've worked too long and too hard to make universal health care a reality in this province. I'm not going to let a doctors strike slow me down. I don't care what you have to do—bring in doctors from England if you have to, and I swear that in five years, the rest of Canada will have followed suit.

(Tommy slams the phone down in the heat of the moment, a determined glint in his eye.)

EXTERIOR. PRAIRIE SCHOOL HOUSE. NIGHT.

(The windows of the little school house are brightly lit from within, surrounded by the vast, dark prairie.)

TOMMY(off-screen): Thanks for coming out tonight, everybody.

INTERIOR. SCHOOL HOUSE. NIGHT.

(A Crowd packed into the school house applauds and starts to disperse. A Burly Man approaches Tommy and doffs his hat respectfully.)

BURLY MAN: Mr. Douglas? I bet you don't remember me, do you, sir?

TOMMY: You do seem familiar, but I do meet an awful lot of people. Refresh my memory.

BURLY MAN: Well, years ago you came to this school and said that you'd see to it that every school in the province would have electricity, and I stood up and said you'd never do it, and, well, here we are standing in the same school house, and it's lit by electric light. I just wanted to say, sir, that I was never so happy to be wrong.

TOMMY: Well, thank you. Thank you. I appreciate it.

(The Burly Man leaves.)

EXTERIOR. SCHOOL HOUSE. NIGHT.

(Tommy steps out on the front stoop. Everyone's gone, and it's quiet. Tommy looks around at the flatness of the prairie and then pulls some keys out of his pocket and gets into the last car in the parking lot. The glinting lights of the car vanish down the road into the distance.)

We apologize that, for reasons beyond our control (time, money, endurance), we are only able to present 11 short films about Tommy Douglas and not the 24 promised in the title. However, given that the actor portraying Mr. Douglas (his grandson, Kiefer Sutherland) is the star of a famous TV program called *24*, we felt the marketing potential far outweighed the glaring inaccuracy of the title.

WHAT'S REAL

Except for Tommy's having a punch-induced dream in the boxing ring, all the of the incidents portrayed above happened, though the verbal exchanges used to convey them are a mixture of fact and fabrication. In a few of the scenes above (less than half), the words spoken by Tommy are attributable to him through interviews or quotations. Regarding the perpetual "glint" described as being in Tommy's eyes, from all accounts he was someone who often, if not always, had a glint in his eye, and so the chance to make a hackneyed cliché out of it was simply too much to resist.

THIRTY-TWO

On to Ottawa

In 1935, Canada was weathering the worst years of the Great Depression. Prime Minister R.B. Bennett had tried a number of different ways to ease the situation, but they all failed. His latest idea had been to set up "Unemployment Relief Camps" for unemployed men. Thousands of men sought relief in the camps, but they were paid only 20 cents per day, had little access to medical attention and were ineligible to vote in federal elections. Things came to a head between April and June of that year when 20,000 workers staged a protest in Vancouver and began the famous "On to Ottawa" trek. The "trekkers" (as they would later become known) piled into railway cars by the thousands and set off for the nation's capital. Among the few blessings of the Great Depression is that there was no reality TV yet, but if there had been…

HOST *(voice-over): This week on* On to Ottawa, *we follow the Trekkies—sorry, the Trekkers, to Regina where leader Arthur "Slim" Evans gets the chance to proceed to the final round in Ottawa.*

(Slim Evans stands in front of a huge crowd in the Exhibition Stadium in Regina.)

SLIM EVANS: We will go on to Ottawa and we will take this fight to old Iron Heel Bennett himself!

(The crowd cheers and shakes their fists over their heads.)

HOST: *But first, let's look back at the weeks that led up to this climactic moment.*

(Scene shifts to the steps of the Vancouver Library with a huge crowd of surging men.)

HOST: *Led by Slim Evans, 20,000 unemployed men drift into Vancouver, eventually occupying the library and leading a march to Stanley Park.*

UNEMPLOYED MAN #1: Iron Heels Bennett won't lift a finger to help us. He just keeps looking for new ways to make sure that the federal government isn't responsible for helping us.

CUT TO:
Bennett addressing the camera.

BENNETT: Well, the problem here is that if we make relief payments too generous, then no one will want to work. Why would they?

CUT TO:
Unemployed Man #2 back in Vancouver

UNEMPLOYED MAN #2: When Bennett was elected, he started a sort of half-assed public works program, but he wanted local municipalities to cover 75 percent of the costs. Well, look around—even big cities like Vancouver can't afford to do that, never mind little towns on the prairies.

CUT TO:
Bennett addressing the camera.

BENNETT: This is just one of those long seasonal slumps that we see from time to time. Canada went through tough times in the 1870s, the 1890s, 1907 to 1908, 1913 to 1915 and 1920 to 1925, but it's always corrected itself. This thing will sort itself out eventually anyhow.

CUT BACK TO:
Unemployed Man #3 in Vancouver.

UNEMPLOYED MAN #3: Then, after a few years when his public works *hadn't,* he switched to just handing out money, but the problem there was that you had to have a permanent address to get it, and all of us were ridin' the rails from town to town lookin' for work. Look how that turned out.

CUT BACK TO:
Bennett addressing the camera.

BENNETT: I'm going to take the recommendations of the military—I'm going to set up work camps, paying the men 20 cents a day. After that, they'll be unlikely to vote for me, so I'm going to deny them the right to vote. *And* to save even *more* money, I'm going to take away their eligibility for

Workman's Compensation. Truthfully, I wasted so much money on the public works program that my priority now is just to balance the federal budget and eliminate the deficit so that investors will regain their confidence.

CUT BACK TO:
Slim Evans in Vancouver.

SLIM EVANS: You've had enough. Canada has had enough. Instead of riding the rails from town to town, now we're going to ride the rails to the nation's capital—On to Ottawa!

(The crowd cheers.)

CUT TO:
Railway cars full of men packed in like cattle.

HOST *(voice-over): And with that, thousands of contestants—sorry, thousands of Trekkers—board railway cars and start their journey across the nation to Ottawa. But when they reach Regina, an unexpected roadblock pops up.*

CUT TO:
Regina train station. Slim Evans stands on train platform and reads telegram to men on train cars.

SLIM EVANS: Bennett has promised to meet with a delegation to hear our demands!

(The crowd cheers.)

SLIM EVANS: But the rest of you will have to stay here.

(The crowd groans.)

HOST *(voice-over): As Slim Evans and seven others head to Ottawa, the RCMP herds the rest of the men into Regina's Exhibition Stadium. Meanwhile, in the nation's capital, Bennett and Slim Evans clash when Bennett accuses Evans of…embezzlement?*

SLIM EVANS: You are a liar. I was arrested for fraudulently converting these funds to feed the starving. I again say you are a liar if you say I embezzled, and I will have the pleasure of telling the workers throughout Canada that I was forced to tell the premier of Canada he was a liar. Don't think you can pull off anything like that. You are not intimidating me a damned bit.

HOST *(voice-over): In spite of his strong words, though, Slim Evans thinks the time may have come to give up—the government just isn't budging. When he gets back to Regina, Evans calls a big rally on July 1 to ask local townsfolk for help, but the Bennett government orders him arrested. Tune in next week for the dramatic series finale of—On to Ottawa!*

SCENES FROM NEXT WEEK'S EPISODE

(Regina street corner. A huge riot is in progress. Police fight the Trekkers, with sticks, stones and whatever other projectiles are ready to hand. A partially dismantled steamroller looms in the foreground. Trekkers pull pieces

off the steamroller and throw them at the police. The
action surges by two hapless cops.)

COP #1: The Trekkers are revolting!

COP #2: Phew! I know—some of them haven't washed for weeks.

COP #1: No, you idiot, I mean they're really revolting.

COP #2: We should have T-shirts made that say, "I was at the Regina Riot and all I got was 20 cents a day."

WHAT'S REAL

The main events portrayed did happen, though I have certainly fabricated all the words used to describe them. The only exception is Slim Evans' tirade to Bennett, which is a direct quote.

The "On to Ottawa" trek was crushed when the Trekkers and their supporters clashed with police in the Regina Rebellion, but Bennett was soundly defeated by William Lyon Mackenzie King in the next election.

THIRTY-THREE

World War II and After

More than 45,000 Canadians died in World War II, and for the survivors, nothing was ever the same. Nor could life go back to normal for the families, friends and loved ones of those who didn't come back. Before Canada entered the war in 1939, amateur "ham" radio operators had proliferated across the country. Ham radio sets operated at very high frequencies, and an operator in Canada could talk to other hams as far away as Europe. When the war began, Canada followed the U.S. blackout on ham communications because of the obvious security implications. The war ended in 1945, and the ham ban was lifted shortly thereafter. Call signs for Canadian operators started with "VE." "VE3" designated an operator in Ontario, and "VE7" designated one in BC, with all of the other provinces having their own individual numbers as well. The following imagines what one such conversation might have been like.

Ham Radio Glossary

CQ: an acronym spoken by a ham operator to indicate that he or she is looking for any contact; this carries over from an old telegraphy practice of tapping out the letters "CQ" as a call to "all stations." No one is quite sure why these letters are used. Although many people assume this code is short for "seek you," it more likely comes from French telegraphy, with the letters "CQ" being code for "Sécurité," which, in this context, means "pay attention."

OM: short for "Old Man," a male ham op

QSL Cards: postcards sent by hams to confirm that voice contact had taken place. QSL cards were usually custom-printed with the user's call letters as well as spaces to write in the date and time the contact had taken places; collecting QSL cards from other operators is a key aspect of ham social life.

QSO: a conversation between two hams

Seventy-three (73): "best regards"; another holdover from the days of the telegraph; in 1857, the number "73" was listed in a telegrapher's manual as meaning "My love to you," but over the intervening years it morphed into something that was more friendly than amorous. Why these particular numbers were chosen seems to be lost in the mists of time.

YL: short for "Young Lady," a female ham op

And finally…

Jerry: slang for German people during World War II. Along with "Fritz," "the Hun," and so forth.

Overheard in the late 1940s

VE7ACK: CQ, this is VE7ACK. CQ, this is VE7ACK. Over.

VE3AUT: VE7ACK, this is VE3AUT. Over.

VE7ACK: VE3AUT! We used to QSO before the war, before the blackout. But you sounded more

like an OM then. Now you sound like quite the YL.
Over.

VE3AUT: I am a YL. I was Bill's YL, and I've taken
over his call sign. Over.

VE7ACK: Oh—I'm Larry. Uh—Over.

VE3AUT: I'm Mabel. Over.

(Static)

VE3AUT: Larry—I'm very sorry to tell you this,
but Bill didn't come back from the war. Over.

VE7ACK: Oh...

VE3AUT: Larry, are you there? Are you there?
Over.

VE7ACK: Oh, sorry—Over.

VE3AUT: He was a pilot—an ace. He got shot
down at the end of the war. He had 13 kills to his
credit. Over.

VE7ACK: Oh...oh...I'm sorry. Look, Mabel,
I'm...I have to go. Over.

VE3AUT: Larry? Larry, are you there? Are you
there? Larry?

—⚬⚬⚬—

VE7ACK: CQ, this is VE7ACK. CQ, this is VE7ACK.
Over.

VE3AUT: VE7ACK, this is VE3AUT. Over.

VE7ACK: Mabel! I've been trying to get in touch with you since last week. I'm sorry I signed off so suddenly, but I was upset about Bill. Over.

VE3AUT: I understand, Larry. A lot of people are. Just after the war I took over his call sign, and I've been trying to talk to all of his old ham friends to let them know. Over.

VE7ACK: You said he was an air ace—I remember he was so proud of having his pilot's licence, and one of the last times I talked to him he said that if war broke out then he was going to volunteer to fly with the RAF. And then war did break out, and we hams were banned from talking with each other. Over.

VE3AUT: I know, Larry. Bill was quite upset when that happened, but he could see why—someone could have talked to Jerry all the way over in Germany. Over.

VE7ACK: And have you found many of Bill's ham friends? Over.

VE3AUT: A few, but mainly I've met other air aces or found out about them. Oh, Larry, there were so many others like Bill—Canadians—lots who came back—lots who didn't. So many names and so many kills that seem to run through my mind, Larry. I found out about Dick Audet from Lethbridge, Alberta, who shot down 11 planes but didn't come back. Russ Bannock shot down 19 buzz bombs headed for England, and he's alive. Charlie Trainor shot down eight planes but spent the rest of the war in a POW camp. And then there are their kids, and I talk to them—oh, Larry, sometimes I think that the kids of the men who didn't come back become hams because they're hoping that one day they'll hear their dads' voices again out of their headphones...

VE7ACK: Did you and Bill have a...little ham? Over.

VE3AUT: No, but I wish we had... Sorry, Larry, I have to go...you shouldn't have to hear me like this.

(Static)

VE7ACK: Mabel, are you there? Over. Mabel?

—◦◦◦—

VE3AUT: VE7ACK, this is VE3AUT. Are you there? VE7ACK, this is VE3AUT. Are you there? Over.

VE7ACK: VE3AUT, this is VE7ACK. Over.

VE3AUT: Larry, sorry I signed off so suddenly last time, but I was getting pretty worked up. Over.

VE7ACK: I understand, Mabel. Don't worry about it. I realized I was so caught up asking about Bill that I never asked about you. How has it been for you since the war ended? Over.

VE3AUT: I hate to say it, but things were actually better for me during the war. Over.

VE7ACK: How do you mean? Over.

VE3AUT: I mean, I had a good job. Over.

VE7ACK: Were you a Bren gun girl? Over.

VE3AUT: I was not a Bren gun girl. But I did meet the Bren gun girl once. She came to visit the factory I worked at. Over.

VE7ACK: What factory did you work at? Over.

VE3AUT: I was an instrument mechanic at the Mosquito factory here in Toronto. Over.

VE7ACK: Who'd have thought de Havilland would come up with a way to build a bomber mostly out of wood? Over.

VE3AUT: I made $30 a week at de Havilland, but since the war's over, all anyone wants to pay is $15 a week and not for being an instrument mechanic, either. I'm supposed to learn to take dictation and answer phones. Over.

VE7ACK: Well, what with women wearing overalls and pants and so forth during the war, we all thought maybe you'd forgotten how to be women. Over.

(Static)

VE7ACK: Mabel? Mabel, are you there? Over.

(More static for a few seconds.)

VE7ACK: Mabel?

—⁓—

VE7ACK: VE3AUT, this is VE7ACK. Do you read me. Over...VE3AUT, this is VE7ACK. Do you read me? Over.

VE3AUT: This is VE3AUT...Over.

VE7ACK: Mabel, look, I'm sorry about what I said about forgetting how to be a woman. Over.

VE3AUT: And? Over.

VE7ACK: It's just that so much has changed since the war. Things we say are different. The things people are thinking are different. What people are willing to believe is different. Why, remember when everyone was saying that our pilots were so good at finding enemy planes in the dark because they ate a lot of carrots? Over.

VE3AUT: Yes, I remember. And it was really radar all along. Over.

VE7ACK: That's right. Even now, you meet people who still think that it was carrots. I guess, maybe, in some other ways, I'm one of those people. Over.

VE3AUT: Oh, that's alright. You know what? Bill thought like that himself. Whenever I sent him a picture of me at the factory, he'd write back and say he just wanted to see me in a dress again. Over.

VE7ACK: Well, can you blame him? He was far away. I know what that's like. I was a medic over there, and, well, when you've seen the things we saw, you kind of just want things to be how they were. Over.

VE3AUT: I know. I'm sorry I never asked you how your war was. Over.

VE7ACK: I don't really like to talk about it so much. Over.

VE3AUT: I see. Say, Larry, I really enjoy these talks we have, and I was wondering if maybe you wouldn't mind sending me a QSL card? Over.

VE7ACK: I'd be happy to send you a QSL card. Will you send one to me? Over.

VE3AUT: I think I will. Over.

VE7ACK: Seventy-three. Over.

VE3AUT: Seventy-three to you, too. Over and out.

QSL card sent by Mabel (VE3AUT) to Larry (VE7ACK). The details of their conversation are listed at the bottom of the card, including the date, time and radio frequency of their discussion. Hams collected each other's QSL cards, which were usually privately printed and showed varying degrees of humour or panache.

WHAT'S REAL

The Canadian air aces mentioned are all real, but the idea of their fatherless children becoming hams in the hopes of their hearing their fathers' voices again is completely fabricated. The working conditions for women described are all true, and there was widespread concern that women would "lose their femininity" (whatever that was supposed to mean) because of doing work that had previously been done by men. After the war, women were expected to take wage cuts and go back to more traditionally "feminine" roles.

Women also featured heavily in war propaganda. Helen Gregory MacGill was the first woman to graduate in electrical engineering in Canada and assumed control of all engineering for production of the Hurricane and Helldiver fighter planes. By far the most famous was Victoria Foster, a.k.a. "The Bren Gun Girl." Generally regarded as Canada's answer to Rosie the Riveter, Foster worked on the assembly line in the factory that produced Bren guns, and she shot to fame after she was photographed posing in front of a completed weapon.

The Mosquito was one of the most versatile aircraft of World War II, designed by the Canadian de Havilland firm and built mostly out of wood. The idea that pilots in the RAF and RCAF were good at locating aircraft during the night because they ate a lot of carrots was a deliberate campaign of misinformation to conceal the fact that British developments in radar had advanced to such a degree that planes could now carry their own radar rigs, called Airborne Interception Radar.

THIRTY-FOUR

The Immigration Years

Starting after the end of World War II in 1945, vast waves of immigrants began to arrive in Canada, laying the foundation for the "multicultural mosaic" that some have chosen to see us as. From 1928 to 1971, the vast bulk of these newcomers arrived by sea and would have first touched Canadian soil at the complex now known as "Pier 21" in Halifax, Nova Scotia. Pier 21 was actually docking facilities for multiple ships (piers 20, 21, 22 and 23) as well as several large buildings called "immigration sheds" all housed on Pier 21. In 2009 it was designated as Canada's National Museum of Immigration.

(A letter from the trustees of Pier 21 to an artist submitting materials to be shown in the museum.)

October 1, 2009

Dear Mrs. LaBrosse:
    On behalf of Pier 21, Canada's Immigration Museum, I would like to thank you for submitting your painting entitled "The Tower of Babel" for our

☞

consideration. Our call for submissions for art to hang in the museum has met with overwhelming response. Although the sheer number of submissions we receive prevents us from responding individually, we are making an exception in your case.

First, your decision to render the scene in the mixed media of wax and oil paint, while artistically daring, is sadly quite impractical. Second, despite our clear instructions to send only photos or copies, you for some reason felt compelled to send the original. Unless you are new to Canada (the possibility of which we cannot discount), you should know that Canada Post is neither the timeliest nor the most gentle of shipping agents.

Combined with your inadvisable decision to ship us the so-called work of art in July (the hottest month of the year), these other factors mean that work itself had already begun to melt before it reached us. It's really a rather ungodly mess at this point, but we think we are still able to make out your original intent and offer the following feedback.

☞

The setting seems to be the interior
of one of the vast "sheds" where arriving immigrants were processed. At centre
is a towering pile of sausages, loaves
of bread, bottles of liquor and other
similar items. We assume that this is
meant to represent the various food-
stuffs that customs agents confiscated
as part of the effort to prevent foot
and mouth disease from gaining a strong-
hold in Canada. We are aware that customs officers really did pile confiscated
items in this manner, but we question
your decision to depict everyone standing around smiling. It was often southern Europeans who brought food with
them—these were people whose lives
and countries were destroyed by World
War II—so we find it unlikely that they
would be standing around and gazing
with glee at food they had, until
recently, looked forward to eating.

It is also unfortunate that, as
a result of your regrettable choice
of media, the faces of most of the
figures have deteriorated into rather
twisted visages of decidedly demonic
mien—perhaps this was your intent, perhaps not. Either way, it is nowhere more
disturbing than the swarm of ghostly

☞

figures hovering near the top of the
painting; we assume these are meant
to represent the British Home Children
shipped to Canada as cheap farm labour
starting in the 1860s. To suggest that
they all died as children and had
nothing better to do than haunt European
immigrants 100 years later is neither
accurate nor fair.

The crowd of emaciated, deranged
women standing to one side, seemingly
with parasitic monsters protruding from
their torsos, we suspect represent the
British war brides and their children.
We must point out that these were usually
among the happier arrivals at Pier 21,
and so their anguished aspect is a mystery to us as is the depiction of their
children as conjoined homunculi—why
not simply show them as rosy-cheeked
babes in arms? However, upon looking
again, perhaps this is what you meant
to portray, but obviously this is not
what comes through at first glance.

On the right-hand side of the painting is group of piratical-looking figures
holding what appear to be tulips and
crouching animalistically beside some
sort of treasure chest. Is this meant to
represent the Dutch? We are aware that,

☞

because of post-war currency restrictions in Holland, many Dutch immigrants converted their money into small, valuable items that they could leave the country with. However, your choice to depict them as tulip-wielding pirates is, again, neither accurate nor fair.

In conclusion, we can commend neither your technique nor your presentation of the subject matter, but we do, nonetheless, thank you for your submission. Perhaps the medium of watercolour is where your talents lie? If you do choose to continue working in this highly unstable mixture of oil paint and wax, then we would point out that Canada Post is probably commissioning new stamps next year, and we strongly encourage you to send your work to them.

Anonymously,
Pier 21, Canada's Immigration Museum

PS: Ordinarily one of us would sign our name to a letter like this, but frankly, the quality of your work was such that no one here feels comfortable with you knowing any of our names.

WHAT'S REAL

All of the groups mentioned in the letter are recognized as major groups to have passed through Pier 21. Children evacuated from London during the Blitz also arrived there, as did many others of refugee status in the years to follow. It should also be noted that almost all Canadian troops going overseas to fight in World War II embarked at Pier 21. And finally, while the painting referred to is completely fictional, the account of the pile of objects confiscated by customs agents is taken directly from Pier 21's website:

Behind long tables immigration personnel directed the newcomers luggage to be put along one wall. Food belonging to the immigrants was confiscated and piled up in a heap in the middle of the hall. Rays of sunshine painted a colourful still life of that mountain of sausages, loaves of bread, wheels of cheeses, fruits and other perishable items.

THIRTY-FIVE

The Cold War Starts at Home

One night in 1945, a cipher clerk from the Russian embassy in Ottawa crammed his briefcase with secret documents and left. His name was Igor Gouzenko, and the documents in his briefcase would prove the existence of a vast Soviet spy ring operating in the Canada, Britain and the U.S. Gouzenko initially had trouble getting anyone to listen to him since Russia was still considered a holdover ally from World War II—no one wanted to "rock the boat." But when Gouzenko finally got people to sit up and listen, the Cold War had begun.

I. Gouzenko's Guide to
BUYING HOUSEHOLD LINENS

Part One: What to look for in a good pillowcase

WHEN MANY COMRADES—sorry, when many Canadians—set out to buy bedding, they often make the mistake of focusing on the sheets and covers. This is all very well if you are planning to actually put the bedding on the bed. But for cipher clerks working abroad

☞

(such as myself), a very different set of considerations must take precedence—in other words, it is the *pillowcases* that will be of the most use to you.

Why is this?

Well, to begin with, if you must hurriedly vacate your apartment in Ottawa because you have just walked out of the Soviet embassy with documents proving the existence of a vast network of Russian spies, the pillowcase is an excellent carryall in which to hastily dump your belongings. You should definitely *not* use a pillowcase when actually sneaking the sensitive documents out of your embassy—this will only attract attention and is, consequently, the very opposite of "clandestine subterfuge." When engaging in this sort of activity, simply use an everyday briefcase, like I did.

A pillowcase stuffed with clothing or other dry goods also comes in handy when you're frantically running around with your wife and kids on the evening of your defection (with secret documents in hand). Since no one will believe what you're telling them—newspaper editors, members of parliament, the RCMP—you and your family are going to be fearfully waiting in a lot of office ante rooms while bumbling bureaucrats ignore you. Having a pillowcase of clothes or other soft items gives your kids something comfortable to rest their troubled brows on while you're on the run.

Undoubtedly though, the pillowcase will be most useful to you in later years when you go public with your story and start appearing on TV. To safeguard your identity from lurking Soviet assassins, take an everyday pillowcase and cut two holes for your eyes, one for your mouth and—presto!—you have a very serviceable mask to keep the prying eyes of the Motherland to themselves.

I prefer to use a newly purchased, plain, white pillowcase straight from the department store, and if you look at the many pictures of me wearing pillowcases, you can see those fresh-out-of-the-package fold lines. This gives me confidence that the pillowcases have not been impregnated with poison dust by the KGB. After all, unless the entire linen department at the Hudson's Bay Company has been infiltrated by *spionem*, I cannot see that I have any-thing to worry about!

In selecting which particular pillowcase to purchase, do not let yourself be sidetracked by bourgeois niceties such as fabric weight and thread count—after all, you are just going to cut holes in it and put it on your head.

As a matter of fact, I often go for the cheapest pillowcase money can buy for the simple reason that I tend to go through rather a lot of them, and they usually only have to last for a couple of TV interviews.

Finally, I should point out that, when travelling in the United States, attiring yourself in such garb as I have described is of dubious wisdom and is almost certain to elicit behaviour in others that leaves one feeling threatened.

And that is it. I hope you have enjoyed my little monograph on pillowcases. In Part Two, we will look at bedsheets and how best to tie them into a knotted rope suitable for escapes involving second- or third-storey defenestration.

WHAT'S REAL

Immediately after he defected, Igor Gouzenko had a great deal of difficulty getting the authorities to act on his information. Starting in the 1950s, he began to appear on TV interviews with a "hood" over his head to conceal his appearance. To all appearances, his "hoods" were pillowcases with holes cut in them.

The humble prose of his guide to buying linen would seem to belie the fact that he was an accomplished writer, winning a Governor General's Award in 1954 for his novel The Fall of Titan, *and also authoring a nonfiction account of his life,* This Was My Choice.

The word spionem *is Russian for "spies."*

THIRTY-SIX

The Diefenbaker Government Scraps the Avro Arrow

In case you haven't heard already, the Avro Arrow was a Canadian-designed and built military aircraft that was at least 20 years ahead of its time. But before the project could come to fruition, the Tory government of John Diefenbaker ("Dief the Chief") cancelled it in 1959.

Top Ten Reasons
John Diefenbaker *Really* Scrapped the Avro Arrow

10. "Sound barrier? What's that, and why should we want to break it?"

9. He thought it was a kind of chocolate bar.

8. Avro refused to call it the "DiefenFighter."

7. 'Cause one day the mint might want to put it on a commemorative quarter, and The Chief is partial to moose.

6. U.S. President Eisenhower skunked him at euchre so Canada had to buy those BOMARC missiles instead.

5. "De Havilland built the Mosquito out of plywood. Why does this one need so much metal?"

4. "Laurier told me to when I sold him that newspaper in 1910."

3. "You talk about losing 30,000 jobs like it's a bad thing."

2. "Once I've signed the NORAD agreement and subordinated Canadian air sovereignty to the Americans, what difference does it make anyway?"

1. "If the Liberals started it, then it must be bad."

WHAT'S REAL

Items #1 and #2 probably come closest to the truth of the matter, with a passing nod to #6.

THIRTY-SEVEN

On the Road
(to the Diefenbunker)
OR
The Subterraneans
(Have Taken Over the Asylum)

Like the rest of the world, from the 1950s to the 1980s, Canada was caught up in the Cold War. While the deluded paranoia of McCarthyism was sweeping the U.S., here at home, we had our own brand of Commie-phobia. The government of the day (John Diefenbaker's Tories) even built underground bunkers so that the Government of Canada could keep governing in the event of a nuclear war (although exactly what or who would be left to govern remains unclear). When word of the bunkers' existence leaked out, the opposition parties immediately labelled the subterranean strongholds "Diefenbunkers."

At the same time that all this suit-and-tie stuff was happening, a comparatively small number of Canadians were exploring the jive-talking world of beat culture in the smoky environs of coffeehouse open stages. You didn't have to like it to listen to it…

Glossary of Hipster Slang

Alabama lie detector: a billy club or cudgel

beating one's gums: talking

bracelets: handcuffs

breakfast uptown: to spend the night in jail

cackle factory: an insane asylum

cubist: a square, in the cultural, rather than the geometric, sense

don't step on no snakes: listen up; get ready; brace yourself

drain the main vein: pee

dime dropper: a snitch, always putting a dime into a payphone to call in his or her treacherous observations

G-men: FBI agents

gat: revolver

Jacko: no, not the late "Wacko Jacko," but rather, the late Jack Kerouac

jerks and fillies, cats and kittens, Eds and Ellas, studs and sisters: ladies and gentlemen

lid: head, noggin'

Ma & Pa Kettle: one's parents, after the *Ma & Pa Kettle* film franchise of the 1940s and '50s

Miltonian: Victorian slang for "police," but used in later years as well

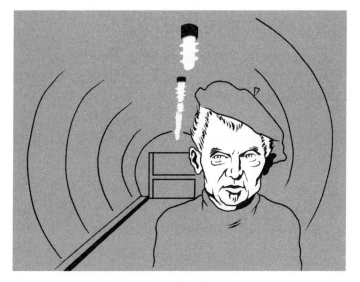

The Diefenbunker is located near Carp, Ontario.

***

packing heat: carrying a gun

Redniks: Russians, communists

Sergeant Preston of the Yukon: a popular American radio/TV program during the 1950s featuring the eponymous Mountie and his dog, King

shaking hands with our bishops: "We're peeing"

soul patch: a small patch of facial hair grown between the lower lip and the chin; worn by all stereotypical beatniks

with my handhood in my man: a spoonerized rendition of "with my manhood in my hand," which can refer to *shaking hands with our bishops* (see above)

One Night in a Coffeehouse (circa 1962)

A HUNDRED CIGARETTES GLOW in the dark, maybe 10 voices
murmur in the crowd, the light is blue, and the
evenin' is cool. Walking onto the stage like a Dharma
Bum comes a Kerouac Wannabe wearing a narrow
suit, wide tie and a soul patch (like Kerouac *never*
had, man).

He has written his rant on a roll of toilet paper,
which his fellow hipster nerds know is because
Jacko wrote *On the Road* on one continuous sheet
of Teletype paper. The question of what writing
a poem on toilet paper says about the poet's self-
worth is left for you and I to ponder.

Whatever words we may think of to describe
this Ray Ban Aviator-eyed, would-be Bohemian,
our doubts are dispelled when his mouth opens,
and the words slide out loose but well meant.

"Jerks and fillies, boys and girls, cats and kittens,
studs and sisters, I stand before you to get behind
some serious trouble we have in this country. Now,
I think all you fine Eds and Ellas, you beautiful
dames and you handsome fellas, I think you think
we have less of the red madness here in Canada than
south of the border. But let me tell you, we have
lots—plenty of people denied because once they
spoke their minds.

"My tale of crazy bafflement starts in the spring-
time. I'm back home in Carp, visiting Ma & Pa Kettle
when me and some other beats drive out into the

country for a little drive and before long we're way out in Nowheresville. So we stop to drain our main veins, and I'm off away from the others staring up at the moon with my handhood in my man, when suddenly there's this flashlight in my eyes, and there's a copper packing heat as he tells me to start beatin' my gums and to tell him what I'm doin' there.

"I sez to him, 'Relax, Miltonian. Me and the other beats are just shaking hands with our bishops, and we'll be off soon. What's all the commotion?' And then I see that we're by this very uncool chain-link fence, and it occurs to me: This is where they're building the government fallout shelter. We've heard rumour in Carp that if the Redniks bomb Nottawa, the Land of Not, this is where the Chief, that's Dief, comes to hunker down—the 'Diefenbunker' me and the other beats call it.

"They say it'll be like an underground hotel with four floors of post-apocalyptic fun built from concrete and fluorescent light, all so that Dief can keep sputtering along. So I sez to the Miltonian, 'Miltonian,' I sez, 'How can you defend our federal Feds with any sort of good conscience after all the Maple Leaf McCarthyism we've so far seen?'

"Now, folks, hold on to your chairs, and don't step on no snakes, 'cause what I'm about to tell you will fry your wigs: it's the tale of Canada's countrywide Commie dragnet. Let's talk about our National Film Board, that be, the NFB. You'd think a film board would be the last place to find witches for hunting, but some cubist at the RCMP—a Sergeant Preston of the Yukon in jackboots and carrying an Alabama lie detector—flimflams his way in and finds a nest of folks at the NFB who are not now, nor had they ever been, communists and gets them fired as well as a raft of others too. Why's that? Could it be that the MP came under some political pressure? Maybe some hints from the Americans that the films we make—what with promoting peace, compassion and truth—might just be anti-American? Ponder that if you will.

"And what about the Ladies Auxiliary in Sudbury? Such nice ladies—they collect dimes in tins for the blind, and you suspect the scarlet creep of communism. Is it that 'CNIB' sounds too much like CCCP to you red-obsessed nudniks? And how did you get your facts anyway? You couldn't have bugged every meeting so you must have had finks and dime droppers all over the place—family, friends and loved ones—all willing to squeal on their family, friends and loved ones. No wonder you gat-packin' G-men are so worried about Commie infiltration when you yourselves have infiltrated so well.

"Then when you were through persecuting the Ladies Auxiliary, you moved on to the Reverend James Endicott. He led the Canadian Peace Congress, preached peace and not war, and refused to button his lip—and in your confused lids, that was a threat? True, he enjoyed receiving his Stalin peace medal and wouldn't even exchange it for a Lenin peace medal, but did you honestly see him leading an insurgent army of…pacifists?

"And what about Gordon Martin in fair BC? Not so fair as it turns out—Comrade Martin, a card-carrying communist and so not allowed to practise law. A World War II vet, gone back to school, passed all his bar exams and not called to the bar. That seems just a little Sovietski in its outlook, *nyet*, boys?

"Or Mr. John Marshall, librarian. Offered a job in Victoria to start up a Bookmobile there but was denied, and why? Because once he had been a member of the Canadian Peace Congress and once he had edited a little rag that "had ties" to a completely different little rag that leaned Left in its outlook on commies. Good ol' Victoria—book-burnin'est gulag in Canada.

"And finally, let us end this sad chapter with the story of Herbert Norman, Canuckian ambassador to Egypt until '57. Author, diplomat and Bryl-haired square, but his views were progressive, and he'd been at Cambridge at the same time as some Limey spies. He was outspoken and yanked the Yankees' chains by refusing to cough up names. He was against fascism, but General MacArthur's right-hand man, General Willoughby, was a fan of fascism and started a file on Norman. Our ambassador fought off an American smear campaign in the 1940s, but when the same trumped-up accusations came 'round again in the '50s, it was all too much, and he threw himself off a rooftop in Cairo. Canadians were angry, sure, but had we, or our government, done anything to stop it? *Nyet, nyet,* Soviet.

"And with that I stopped talking and looked at the G-man. I hoped he wasn't going to hit me with his Alabama lie detector or plug me with his gat. But instead he took out the bracelets and slapped them on me. Well, I thought to myself, it's either the cackle factory or the big house for me. It was the latter; the G-man and some other spooks lurking in the trees gave me and the other beats breakfast uptown and then let us out the next day. Guess we should count ourselves lucky they didn't accuse us of being commies for speaking our minds."

WHAT'S REAL

There really was a Diefenbunker built in Carp, Ontario (just outside of Ottawa), and at the time of this writing, it is open to the public as a Cold War museum. Aside from the anonymous narrator getting busted for peeing on the fence, all of the events referred to are well documented—the NFB purges, the persecution of the Sudbury Ladies' Auxiliary, the surveillance of the Reverend James Endicott, the denial of Gordon Martin's rights, the apparent black-listing of John Marshall and, finally, the sad demise of Herbert Norman.

THIRTY-EIGHT

The Munsinger Affair

All but forgotten (except to Canadians of "a certain age"), Gerda Munsinger was at the centre of one of Canada's very few sex scandals (at least one of the few that anyone can remember). Nothing was really at stake except for the reputations of those involved, but there you have it—this is Canada, after all.

HERITAGE MCMOMENT #5

FROM: Richard Wanker
Broadcast Executive
Historical TV Channel

TO: Mordant Wit
Freelance Writer

Hi again Mordant,
    For our final Heritage McMoment
this year, we've decided to do something a little special—a look at the
Munsinger Affair. I have to be honest.
I'd never even heard of it until I was

☞

surfing around on the web and discovered
that it was one of Canada's only political sex scandals. I was really surprised
because I didn't even think that Canadians had sex, much less Canadian politi-
cians, and frankly, if they do, I wish
they wouldn't—I don't like to think
about it.

Also, I've started trying to think
the way you do, and I'm at a loss as to
why this is in anyway important, other
than that—like I say—it was a sex
scandal, and those are few and far
between in Canada, at least good ones
are.

I've really enjoyed working with you
and hope we can collaborate together
again in the near future.

Yours truly,
Richard (Dick) Wanker

Heritage McMoment #5:
The Munsinger Affair

Suggestions for visuals: I think we'd see the reporter character knocking on a door in the hallway of a 1960s apartment building, and then we'd see inside the apartment as he talks to Munsinger.

TITLE

West Germany, 1966

(A well-dressed reporter knocks on an apartment door in a hallway.)

REPORTER

Ms. Munsinger? Ms. Munsinger? Will you talk to me? I'm from the *Toronto Star.*

(The door opens to reveal Gerda Munsinger, a hot German Fräulein.)

MUNSINGER

I suppose you want to ask about Sévigny.

(The reporter is in Munsinger's apartment frantically scribbling as Gerda speaks.)

WRITER'S NOTES

Dear Dick Wanker—I quit.

I fully understand how someone as appallingly ignorant as you has risen to your position—it's called "failing upwards," and it happens a lot in television and sometimes in advertising as well.

But what I don't understand is why you think you can write. The first half of this thing is OK, but what I'm talking about is the incredibly long voice-over by the Narrator at the end—how stupid are you? Have you not been paying attention to any of the other Heritage McMoments you've "written"? It's way too long.

☞

NARRATOR

And that was how
the world found out
that Gerda Munsinger,
a West German prosti-
tute, had slept with John
Diefenbaker's associate
minister of defence,
Pierre Sévigny. A breach
of security? Probably
not. But a Canadian
Heritage McMoment?
Definitely. Did we men-
tion that she may have
also been doing the nasty
with the minister of
transport, George Hees?
It was nearly 50 years
ago, so who really cares
anyway? I mean, it's not
like she was performing
in the half-time show at
the Super Bowl and we
accidentally got to see
her nipple—now there's
a sex scandal!

Heritage McMoments:
history as we wish it had
happened.

*What visuals were you plan-
ning to use to show Munsinger
and Sévigny sleeping together?
Unless you were planning to
air this thing on the CanAdult
Network, it's going to get
pretty boring watching
Munsinger talking to the
Reporter and the Reporter
writing it all down and
Munsinger talking some more
and the Reporter writing it
all down.*

*Don't ask questions like,
"Who cares anyway?" when
you yourself clearly don't
know the answer.*

*And why are you going on
about Janet Jackson and her
"wardrobe malfunction" at the
Super Bowl? It has nothing
to do with your topic.*

Like I said—I quit!

FROM: Richard Wanker, Broadcast Executive
Historical TV Channel

TO: Mordant Wit, Freelance Writer

Hi Mordant,

Sorry, but I haven't read any of
your notes on my last script because
I've just been promoted to Broadcast
Executive in Charge of Production for
the entire Network—very exciting!

Anyway I just wanted to drop you
a line to let you know how much I've
enjoyed working with you—I've learned
a lot, and I hope you did, too! Maybe
we can do it again some time.

Sincerely,
Richard (Dick) Wanker

WHAT'S REAL

Gerda Munsinger did have affairs with the two men named and was discovered by a Toronto Star *reporter years after the fact. But instead of having her story commemorated with a* Heritage Minute, *many of the details emerged during a debate in Parliament and later in a 1966 episode of the CBC news program* This Hour Has Seven Days.

THIRTY-NINE

1967: The Last Good Year
OR
Marshall McLuhan: The Tutorial He Never Gave

As a sort of birthday present for Canada's centennial year in 1967, the international community chose Montréal as the location of that year's World Fair, to be called Expo '67 (the city that had been the first choice—Moscow—had backed out). That year was also a busy one for Marshall McLuhan, a Canadian regarded by many as the pre-eminent media theorist of the 20th century. (If the second half of the preceding sentence makes no sense to you, just skip this chapter—you're nearly at the end of the book anyhow, and if you haven't figured out who the murderer is by this point, you're probably not going to.) McLuhan's most famous notions are that "the medium is the message" as well as the idea of a "global village." He also may or may not have invented the term "surfing" (as in the Internet), even though the Internet's rise would not happen for almost another 30 years.

May 1967

(A lecture hall somewhere on the University of Toronto campus. The lecture hall is abuzz with excited, youthful voices. McLuhan enters to scattered applause.)

MCLUHAN: Does anyone here know the name of the first telephone Pole?

(Uncertain silence.)

MCLUHAN: Alexander Graham Kowalski.

(Disbelieving and slightly dismayed silence)

MCLUHAN: When is baseball first mentioned in the Bible?

(Uncomfortable and baffled silence)

MCLUHAN: When Rebecca goes to the well with a pitcher.

(Stage whisper from the back of the room: Is this guy for real?)

MCLUHAN: Canada! What is our place in the world? Canada is a nation that did not have a 20th century—we seem to have leapt from the 19th century directly into the opening years of the 21st.

STUDENT #1: But it's just after the middle of the 20th century. How can you say that?

MCLUHAN: I say it by forming my mouth into a series of shapes that produce phonemes and epiglottal stops—that's how I say it.

STUDENT #2: Dr. McLuhan, you're famous for the idea that the medium is the message. If that is true, what do this year's centennial celebrations say about Canada?

MCLUHAN: I've since refined that to say that every new medium creates its own environment, and that environment, in turn, acts on human sensibilities in a total and ruthless fashion.

STUDENT #2: OK, fine, so what does that say about the centennial?

MCLUHAN: You're suggesting then that the centennial is, itself, a medium for the transmission of content, and I suppose in one sense you're right. The Expo '67 site in Montréal is on an island that we have constructed for it—but here I would argue that we have constructed the environment—it has not constructed us, or rather impacted on our sensibilities, such as would happen with a true medium for the transmission of content.

STUDENT #3: Well, then, if we've created an island as the medium for our message, what does that say about Canada's place in the world today?

MCLUHAN: It utterly confirms what I said before about Canada seeming to have skipped the 20th century, and that's what I mean when I say Canada is a backward country—we were born in the 19th century and we largely seem to have stayed there. I think it gives Canada a vantage point from which to view world events without really participating in them, watching them as show business really. What better place to observe from than an island in the middle of a river moving swiftly on either side of it?

STUDENT #4: That pavilion they've built for Expo—Habitat they call it—looks like a giant Habitrail set for hamsters like the one my little sister has.

MCLUHAN: There it is then—we've built the construct of an enclosure that lets us contain the rest of the world for observation much as a child looks in on the daily doings of pet hamsters or gerbils.

(Laughter)

STUDENT #1: Dr. McLuhan, I have some friends who were in San Francisco a while ago, and they swear they saw you in a…in a topless restaurant there. Is that true?

MCLUHAN: The place has no windows, so if they saw me there, they must have been inside themselves.

(More laughter)

MCLUHAN: But, yes, it's true—I think the newspapermen I was with were trying to embarrass me by taking me there, but it didn't work. I merely observed that, in lieu of actual clothing, the waitresses there wore their clients like—

STUDENT #1: Like flesh tuxedos?

MCLUHAN: Metaphorically, yes—they wore us as extensions of their skin in the sense that we, their patrons, became their environment, as opposed an environment of, say, clothing.

(General murmurs of understanding and approval)

STUDENT #5: Hey, McLuhan, I saw you on a CBC interview the other week where you said that you did *not* think that radio and TV and the other electronic media would turn us into tribal automatons, but I disagree. I think that's the inherent evil of this stuff. George Orwell got it wrong when he said Big Brother would be watching us—really, we watch Big Brother, and that's what's so insidious about it...we gape at our false electronic gods so they can feed us the myths of soap companies and car manufacturers.

MCLUHAN: I take it even further than that—I think Big Brother is actually inside of us, as we become our own observers. But, no, I for one don't believe that we will become tribal automatons, because media like TV demand total involvement—they create a total field of instant awareness.

STUDENT #5: Awareness of what? New kinds of dish detergent? They don't make us more involved—they turn us into zombies, each in our little cell watching our little glowing box.

MCLUHAN: You only think that because you have never truly considered these matters. Next question.

STUDENT #1: Hey, McLuhan, have you ever taken LSD?

MCLUHAN: No, I haven't, but I have read *Finnegan's Wake* aloud, and people who have taken LSD have told me that the experience is pretty much the same.

STUDENT #6: Dr. McLuhan, one of your main tenets is that we can learn a great deal about something by observing its effects—

MCLUHAN: That's right. For example, in England, one of the effects of central heating was to make people much more interested in windows because you could open them to let out the excess heat or draw the blinds to keep it in or just simply gaze outward, happy to contemplate the withering elements since now the threat of their effect on you was negated by...central heating.

STUDENT #7: So...like, how if our skulls were made of lead, floors would be much more decorative?

(Laughter)

MCLUHAN: That's exactly what I'm saying, but I don't discount the possibility that your skulls *are* made of lead.

(More laughter)

STUDENT #6: So, in observing the effects of radio and TV, what I see are people engaging less with each other, and more with the media. You have said in the past, perhaps flippantly, that one reason you do not like to drive is that you refuse to be a mere servo mechanism to the car; that is, you are merely producing motion and force in servitude to the car, but with transistor radios becoming smaller and smaller, and TVs, too, don't you think that we run the risk of eventually becoming servo mechanisms for our media? Simply biological servants whose purpose is to carry our electronic devices from place to place so that they can carry out their business?

(Long pause)

MCLUHAN: You know…I hadn't thought of that.

(McLuhan gazes off into space, lost in thought. Eventually the students file out into the late '60s afternoon sunshine.)

WHAT'S REAL

Believe it or not, this is probably not far off from what it was like to hear Marshall McLuhan speak, though this version is much, much shorter. McLuhan was known for his love of awful puns and reportedly did begin talks with a few usually irrelevant jokes, before moving on to elaborate analogies and metaphors that drove actual experts crazy with their numerous inaccuracies and unproven assumptions.

The two jokes included here are known to have been told by him. His views that Canada seems to have skipped the 20th century were spoken by McLuhan on a CBC TV interview from 1967. I was unable to discover his actual views on the site of Expo '67 in Montréal.

McLuhan was taken to a topless restaurant in San Francisco and did make the reported observation.

☞

His optimistic hopes for the effects of TV (especially) and other electronic media are also widely known and crop up in the same CBC interview already mentioned and in the sources at the back of this book. He did believe that a form of George Orwell's "Big Brother" (from his novel, 1984) existed inside us all, but the notion that we watch Big Brother (instead of the other way around) is, as far as I know, my own.

His views on LSD and Finnegan's Wake *are also from the CBC interview. McLuhan did feel that one could learn more about a thing by observing the effect it had on people than by observing the thing itself, and his statement about central heating and windows was made by him while he was studying in England.*

Finally, it is difficult to know what he would have made of the advent of the Sony Walkman, let alone the Internet, mobile devices and MP3 players. His assumption that the new media would cause people to be more involved in the world around them seems, to this writer, sadly mistaken.

FORTY

The National Energy Program

Regarded nowadays as possibly the worst idea Pierre Trudeau ever had (and there were many), the National Energy Program (NEP) is still regarded as a pivotal moment in the development of so-called Western Alienation in Canada. But what if it had been a TV show? From 2004 to 2009, Corner Gas was one of Canada's most successful sitcoms (insert your own oxymoron joke here). It centred on the staff and regulars at Corner Gas, the last gas station for 65 kilometres on the Saskatchewan prairies. What better metaphor for the National Energy Program?

(A pastiche in six scenes)

Cast of Characters

Bent: The owner of Prairie Petrol, the only gas station for 65 kilometres, in the small town of Gusher, Alberta

David: Half of Gusher's local police force

Ditzy: Mayor of Gusher

Emily: Bent's long-suffering mother who sees things as they are and tells it how it is

Frank: The local layabout, rarely employed and less often right

Kelly: The other half of the police force

Omar: Bent's obstreperous father who has only a tenuous grasp of the facts

Stacey: The owner of a family diner, The Gem, attached to Prairie Petrol. She's from Toronto.

Wendy: Bent's overeducated and slightly cynical employee

INTERIOR. GAS STATION. DAY

(Bent and Wendy stand at the counter of Prairie Petrol. Bent reads a comic. Wendy reads a thick textbook. Frank enters through the doors and stands in front of the counter.)

FRANK: Have you heard about the National Energy Program?

BENT: Is it another phone-in show on the CBC?

WENDY: Actually, it's a grossly unfair—some would say punitive—program that Prime Minister Trudeau has introduced.

FRANK: Trudeau—he's Ben Mulroney's dad, right?

BENT: As long as I don't have to listen to people on the radio phoning in to talk about turning off lightbulbs, I don't see how it could be that bad.

WENDY: Then how do you feel about the federal government taking 25 percent of all oil-based revenues?

BENT: That's just the kind of thing I expect the federal government to do.

FRANK: This Trudeau guy—did he come into my bedroom and then leave again?

BENT: He wouldn't come into your bedroom in the first place.

WENDY: Alright, Bent, then how do you feel about selling oil to the rest of Canada at well below the world price?

BENT: Like the man said, just watch me.

WENDY: It actually means you lose money.

BENT: Again, just watch me.

(Stacey enters from the back of the store. She's wrapped in a blanket.)

STACEY: It's freezing over at the restaurant. Hey, I'm from Toronto, can I borrow a cup of oil?

(Bent, Wendy and Frank glare at her.)

OPENING TITLES AND THEME

> *"You can tell me that your oil went away*
>
> *But don't you worry, baby, that's OK*
>
> *'Cause we'll squeeze every drop*
>
> *We'll steal every buck*
>
> *You payyyyyyyy!*

There's not a lot you can do

Think again, baby, that's not true

That's why you can stick it to the man

With the National Energy Program."

INTERIOR. OMAR AND EMILY'S HOUSE. DAY.

(Emily sits at the kitchen table drinking a cup of tea. Omar barges in with a bumper sticker and holds it out.)

OMAR: My new bumper sticker.

(Emily doesn't even turn to look at him.)

EMILY: What's it say?

OMAR: "Let those Easter Jackasses Freeze in the Dark!"

EMILY: It's not "Easter," it's "Eastern."

OMAR: I don't care if they're Piscapolian, they're still freezing.

EMILY: Do you even understand what this is about?

OMAR: Sure, it's about…well, jackasses, and they're…eastern, and it's dark and they're…freezing.

EMILY: Exactly how far east do you think it means?

OMAR: Well, China and Japan and—you know—countries like Hawaii!

EMILY: Aloha, Don Ho.

EXTERIOR. OIL FIELD. DAY.

(Kelly and David pull up in their squad car.)

WIDE ANGLE

(Ditzy, the mayor, is standing beside a single, small oil derrick with a drill.)

DAVID: Got a permit for this drilling operation?

DITZY: I'm the mayor! Do I need a permit?

KELLY: We have to make sure that your company is at least 50-percent Canadian owned.

DITZY: Well, I own the land, and I do all the work, but my cousin in Japan sent me the drilling set-up as a Christmas present.

DAVID: How much is the land worth?

DITZY: I haven't found oil yet, so not really all that much.

KELLY: Is the equipment worth more than the land?

DITZY: Probably.

DAVID: Then, since the equipment's the property of your cousin in Japan, that means you're less than 50-percent Canadian owned.

KELLY: We have to write you a ticket.

DITZY: This is so complicated—I don't understand.

DAVID: It's like if the Klingons found dilithium crystals on Romulus—

KELLY: Please don't turn this into a *Star Trek* thing.

EXTERIOR. GAS STATION PUMPS. DAY.

(A car drives off. Wendy is waving goodbye.)

WENDY: Thanks. Come again.

BENT: That was pretty cheap for a full tank of gas.

WENDY: It's this new "Made-in-Canada" price that the government made you adopt.

BENT: About that—I'm losing so much money selling gas for less than it costs anywhere else that I'm going have to let you go.

WENDY: That's not fair—I was made in Canada.

BENT: Well, there you go—that means I can hire you back, but I can't pay you as much.

WENDY: I see—so the state has no place in bedrooms of the nation, but it can stick its head up our gas pumps whenever it wants.

BENT: Your words, not mine.

INTERIOR. THE GEM. DAY.

(Stacey huddles behind the snack counter in her blanket. Omar and Emily enter through the restaurant door. Omar speaks to Stacey.)

OMAR: This is all your fault because of that trip you took to Hawaii.

STACEY: I've never been to Hawaii.

OMAR: See? If you had, you wouldn't be so cold now.

STACEY *(looking at Emily):* What is he talking about?

EMILY: He's mad because everyone else is mad. It's this National Energy Program thing.

STACEY: Well, it's cheap gas—what am I supposed to do? Not buy it?

EMILY: The fact that you're buying it, combined with the fact that you're from Toronto, really gets our goat.

STACEY: But the National Energy Program is mainly to benefit the Maritimes.

EMILY: Whatever. If you're from east of Manitoba, as far as we're concerned, you're a spiteful, arrogant snob.

OMAR: Toronto, Newfoundland, Hawaii—the Axis of Oil.

EMILY: Now even I don't know what you're talking about.

OMAR: You and whose army?

EXTERIOR. GAS PUMPS. DAY.

(Stacey pulls up in her car. Bent emerges from the store and approaches the car.)

STACEY: Hey, Bent. Can I get some more of that cheap gas?

BENT: Sorry, but I'm losing so much money that I had to stop selling gas.

STACEY: Well, I don't care—I'll pay full price if I have to—it's gas.

BENT: Yeah, but the government says I can only sell it to the rest of Canada at the low price.

STACEY: So we both lose, and now the NEP appeals equally to no one.

BENT: Just like all those compelling dramas the CBC makes.

INTERIOR. PRAIRIE PETROL. DAY.

(Bent and Wendy stand behind the counter. Frank enters.)

FRANK: Hey, did you hear?

WENDY: You got kicked off the EI ski team?

FRANK: I can't ski. No, this new prime minister, Brian TheLooney or whatever—he's dismantling the National Energy Program.

BENT: And not a moment too soon.

FRANK: If he's dismantling it, what do you think they'll do with the parts?

BENT: Probably build an Air Bus.

FRANK: Hey, if it's an Air Bus, how does it stop to pick people up?

WENDY: I think I feel a Goods and Services Tax coming on.

ROLL END CREDITS.

WHAT'S REAL

All of the unfavourable conditions Bent is subjected to were imposed on prairie oil sellers. There were bumper stickers that said, "Let those Eastern bastards freeze in the dark." The situation came to a head when Alberta premier Peter Lougheed announced that his province would cease selling oil to the rest of Canada, which forced the federal government to negotiate a slightly more favourable agreement.

Economists estimate that the NEP cost Alberta between $50 billion and $100 billion in direct revenue. Brian Mulroney's government dismantled the NEP in 1986.

FORTY-ONE

The CanadArm

The CanadArm is a 50-foot-long mechanical arm that has been used in space shuttle missions since 1981. In spite of its spelling, which means it should be pronounced "Cana–DARM," many people actually say "Canada Arm." Not exactly the sexiest name out there, but of course it had to reflect Canada's proud position as butler to the U.S., and so we can only imagine what wildly inappropriate suggestions people might have made as to what it ought to be called. If the namers were well versed in Canadian current affairs, French Canadian films, as well as future prime ministers and comedians not yet well known, this might have been the list they came up with.

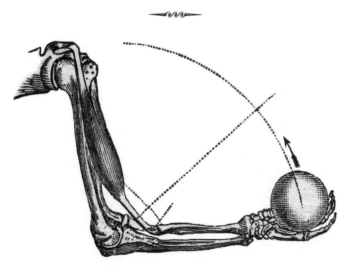

An early design for the CanadArm that was later discovered to be a photocopy out of some old encyclopedia

Top Ten
· Rejected Names for the CanadArm

10. The Trudeau Appendage

9. The Honourable Member

8. The Swivelling Manipulator
   (a.k.a. The Mulroney-grabbing Apparatus)

7. The Canada Shaft

6. Northern Elbow

5. CanadArmed and Dangerous

4. The True North Groper

3. The Maple Leaf Erector

2. Mon Robotic Arm Antoine

1. Jim Carry

WHAT'S REAL

I made the whole list up, but Pierre Trudeau and Brian Mulroney were prime ministers of Canada; Mon Oncle Antoine is a 1971 French Canadian Film; and Jim Carrey (not "Carry") is a famous movie star from Canada.

FORTY-TWO

The Ghosts of Stephen Harper: Past, Present and Future

Long before he was from Alberta, Stephen Harper was from Toronto, where he belonged to the Young Liberal Club at his high school, Richview Collegiate. However, he disagreed so strongly with the National Energy Program that he defected to the Progressive Conservatives. He also appeared on Reach for the Top, *a TV game show for Canada's top high school students. It is unclear whether any video footage of Harper's appearance survives, and if it does, whether anyone other than Harper himself is allowed to look at it.*

In Harper's days as Opposition leader, there was much talk of his supposed "secret agenda" that presumably contained all kinds of deranged right-wing objectives to be enacted once he came to power; we examine that idea here as well.

And finally, Prime Minister Harper's plans to allow the self-employed to contribute to and collect EI were overshadowed by a series of unfortunate photo-ops in which Tory MPs were shown presenting gigantic novelty cheques bearing not the Government of Canada logo, but that of the Conservative Party of Canada (this, despite representing government funds). Read on ...

The Ghost of Harper Past

If Harper as a high school student was anything like Harper the prime minister, his appearance on *Reach for the Top* may have played out like what follows.

HOST: This week on *Reach for the Top,* Richview Collegiate challenges Vincent Massey Collegiate. Four students from each school compete for the chance for their team to advance to the finals. Now, to start, we have the "shooter" questions, which means any student from any team can answer—

STEVE: Excuse me, but I'll be the only one doing any answering for my team.

HOST: Ah, one of the students from Richview has something to say.

STEVE: Yes, I'm not allowing anyone to answer from my team except me. You see, I'm smarter than all of them, and they might say something that is either incorrect or just embarrassing.

HOST: Well, Steve…Harper, is it? Steve, there are no leaders on this show—all students are equal.

STEVE: Well, I'm at the head of my class so I've decided that I'm the leader.

HOST: You won't be able to stop them from answering if they want to. OK, now to begin with the questions—

STEVE: I'm not answering any questions unless they've been submitted in advance, and, furthermore, I get to choose who *asks* the questions.

HOST: Giving contestants the questions in advance would defeat the purpose of the game—

STEVE: Yes, it would defeat the purpose of the game, but it would allow me to achieve my goals, which are far more important to me than openness or transparency.

HOST: And as for choosing who asks the questions, I'm the only host here, so it's going to be me.

STEVE: We'll see about that—maybe someone will buy up their own string of hosts to ask me the questions I want. After all, you current hosts have a monolithically liberal and feminist agenda.

HOST: What the hell are you talking about?

———

The Ghost of Harper Present

Here we imagine the late-night doodlings on napkins that may portend what the future has to offer.

The Real Secret Agenda

1. Rename the CanadArm to the "ConservaTron 3000" (or maybe "The Stevinator").

2. Change the Canadian flag design to include blue sidebars and the Conservative "C" logo instead of red sidebars and leftist red maple leaf.

3. Introduce legislation to make all Canadians wear pins with the Conservative logo.

4. Send Canadian/Conservative troops to Iraq. It's never too late!

5. See to it that that George W. Bush replaces the Queen on the loonie, leading to the new nickname, The Bushy.

6. Eliminate all political parties in Canada except one.

7. ~~Blow the budget surplus those corrupt Liberals left behind.~~ DONE!

8. Redefine rules of Parliament so that less than half is a majority.

9. Create a pipeline of pneumatic tubes (just like at Home Depot!) to funnel stimulus funds directly to Conservative constituencies.

10. Issue decree for immediate revival of the following 1970s TV shows: *The Star Lost, The Trouble with Tracy* and *The Joyce Davidson Show*—this was truly the Golden Age of Canadian TV!

The Ghost of Harper Future

What will happen when Harper is blessedly out of a job and applying for EI benefits? Perhaps something along these lines.

EI OFFICER: I see that you're applying for Employment Insurance benefits, is that right?

HARPER: You didn't submit that question in advance so I won't be able to answer.

EI OFFICER: Your occupation is listed here as "prime minister."

HARPER: Correct.

EI OFFICER: Prime minister of…?

HARPER: Canada.

EI OFFICER: I see. I'm afraid that's not a sector or trade that we recognize as legitimate employment.

HARPER: OK, look, I had a job with the federal government—a government job—and those EI deductions have been coming off for a while now.

EI OFFICER: Yes, I'm just looking through your file here. You say you had a job with the federal government and your position was prime minister. Now, to my way of thinking, if you have a government job and you're the leader of the government, then you are, *ipso facto*, self-employed.

HARPER: Technically, the Queen is the head of the government so I was working for her, as an employee of her government.

EI OFFICER: Yes, well the Queen isn't the one applying for benefits here.

HARPER: Besides, we opted to offer EI benefits to the self-employed.

EI OFFICER: Well, which is it? Were you self-employed or not?

HARPER: You didn't submit that question in advance and so I'm not answering.

EI OFFICER: Either way, we have some compelling evidence that you've been working under the table since you left office, and so you may have some undeclared income.

HARPER: What do you mean?

EI OFFICER: Well, I have this advertisement from a catalogue that seems to suggest you've been moonlighting as an underwear model in 1920s British Columbia.

HARPER: What? Let me see that….This is a catalogue from 1928! How could I be in a catalogue more than 30 years before I was even born? And, besides, this is just a sketch, and it doesn't even look that much like me.

EI OFFICER: Alright, Mr. Harper, we'll process your claim, and if you are eligible for benefits, you can expect to receive a giant novelty cheque with the Conservative Party logo on it sometime soon.

HARPER: But that's worthless.

EI OFFICER: Next!

In the future, will Stephen Harper be a time-travelling underwear model? This disturbing image from a 1928 dry goods catalogue offers strong evidence to support such a hypothesis.

WHAT'S REAL

Harper did appear on Reach for the Top. *To understand the cryptically foreshadowing statement he makes at the end, it is necessary to know that, in later years, Harper would praise Conrad Black's purchase of the Southam newspaper chain because it would finally put an end to what Harper called its "monolithically liberal and feminist" approach.*

Regarding the "secret agenda," we are not sure what Harper's TV watching habits may be, but The Star Lost *was a terrible Canadian sci-fi show;* The Trouble with Tracy *is widely regarded as one of the worst sitcoms ever made; and* The Joyce Davidson Show *was a one-on-one chat program so deservedly forgotten that, at the time of writing, it doesn't even have an entry on* Wikipedia.

As for the section where Harper applies for EI benefits, it is the one section of this book that looks not to a fabled past, but rather, a brighter future.

Notes on Sources

PUTTING THE *INUK* IN *INUKSHUK*
Carter, A. (Ed.). *The Virago Book of Fairy Tales.* London, England: Virago Press, 1991.

SO-CALLED POTLATCHING
http://en.wikipedia.org/wiki/Potlatch

THE NORSE IN NEWFOUNDLAND
Magnusson, M. and H. Palsson (Trans.). *The Vinland Sagas: The Norse Discovery of North America.* London, England: Penguin Classics, 1st printing, 1965.

http://en.wikipedia.org/wiki/L%27Anse_aux_Meadows

EARLY EXPLORERS OF CANADA
Ferguson, W. *Canadian History for Dummies,* 2nd ed. Mississauga, ON: John Wiley & Sons, 2005.

HENRY HUDSON
Ferguson, *Canadian History for Dummies.*

LES FILLES DU ROI
Ferguson, *Canadian History for Dummies.*

http://en.wikipedia.org/wiki/Filles_du_roi

NEW FRANCE PLAYS ITS CARDS RIGHT
Hurley-Rutherford, P. *True North Strange and Free.* Montréal, QC: The Reader's Digest Association (Canada), 2002.

www.bankofcanada.ca/en/dollar_book/1600-170.pdf

THE FIGHT FOR THE FUR TRADE

Campbell, M. Wilkins. *The Nor'Westers: The Fight for the Fur Trade*. Toronto, ON: Macmillan and Canada, 1974.

Ferguson, *Canadian History for Dummies*.

http://en.wikipedia.org/wiki/Fur_trade

THE ACADIAN EXPULSION

Ferguson, *Canadian History for Dummies*.

http://en.wikipedia.org/wiki/Acadian_Expulsion

THE BATTLE OF THE PLAINS OF ABRAHAM

Anderson, F. *Crucible of War*. New York: Alfred A. Knopf, 2000.

Ferguson, *Canadian History for Dummies*.

Hibber, C. *Wolfe at Québec*. London, England: Longmans, Green & Co, 1959.

Stacey, C.P. and D.E. Greaves (Eds.). *Québec, 1759: The Siege and the Battle*. Toronto, ON: Robin Brass Studio, 2002.

http://en.wikipedia.org/wiki/Battle_of_the_plains_of_Abraham

http://www.cbc.ca/canada/montreal/story/2009/02/17/mtl-plains-battle-cancelled-0217.html

PETER POND DISCOVERS THE ALBERTA TAR SANDS

Le Riche, T. *Alberta's Oil Patch: The People, Politics & Companies*. Edmonton, AB: Folklore Publishing, 2006.

http://www.eoearth.org/article/Athabasca,_Alberta

ALEXANDER MACKENZIE'S VOYAGE TO THE PACIFIC

Mackenzie, A. (Walter Sheppe, Ed.). *Journal of the Voyage to the Pacific*. New York: Dover Publications, 1995.

THE CURIOUS CASE OF JOHN FUBBISTER

Harding, L. *The Journeys of Remarkable Woman: Their Travels on the Canadian Frontier.* Kitchener, ON: Upney Editions, 1994.

http://www.biographi.ca/009004-119.01-e.php?&id_nbr=2441

http://www.hbc.com/hbcheritage/history/people/women/iso-belgunn.asp

THE EARL OF SELKIRK'S EXCELLENT MISADVENTURES (1805–18)

Campbell, *The Nor'Westers.*

Ferguson, *Canadian History for Dummies.*

Richmond, R and T. Villemaire. *Colossal Canadian Failures: A Short History of Things that Seemed Like a Good Idea at the Time.* Toronto, ON: Dundurn Press, 2002.

http://en.wikipedia.org/wiki/Lord_Selkirk

http://en.wikipedia.org/wiki/Red_River_Colony

FRANKLIN'S LOST EXPEDITION: THE PREQUEL (1819–22)

http://en.wikipedia.org/wiki/Coppermine_Expedition_of_1819

OUR SPACE INVADERS

Ferguson, *Canadian History for Dummies.*

ROSE FORTUNE

Michaelides, M. *Renegade Women of Canada: The Wild, Outrageous, Daring and Bold.* Edmonton, AB: Folklore Publishing, 2006.

http://en.wikipedia.org/wiki/Act_Against_Slavery

http://en.wikipedia.org/wiki/Front_Page_Challenge

http://www.annapolisheritagesociety.com/hinotablerose.htm

MARY ANN SHADD

Forster, M. *100 Canadian Heroines: Famous and Forgotten Faces.*
Toronto, ON: Dundurn Press, 2004.

http://en.wikipedia.org/wiki/Mary_Ann_Shadd

CORNELIUS KRIEGHOFF

http://en.wikipedia.org/wiki/Cornelius_Krieghoff

http://www.biographi.ca/009004-119.01-e.php?&id_nbr=5079

REPRESENTATION BY POPULATION

Ferguson, *Canadian History for Dummies.*

CUTTING CANADA'S BORDER

Butler, R. *Vanishing Canada.* Toronto & Vancouver: Clarke,
Irwin & Company, 1980.

http://en.wikipedia.org/wiki/Aroostook_War

http://en.wikipedia.org/wiki/Canadian_border

http://en.wikipedia.org/wiki/Oregon_boundary_dispute

http://en.wikipedia.org/wiki/Pig_war

THE CARIBOO GOLD RUSH

Hollihan, T. *Gold Rushes.* Edmonton, AB: Folklore Publishing,
2001.

http://en.wikipedia.org/wiki/Cariboo_camels

THE CHARLOTTETOWN CONFERENCE

Pratt, T.K. *Dictionary of Prince Edward Island English.* Toronto,
ON: University of Toronto Press. 1996.

Waite, P.B. *The Life and Times of Confederation 1864–1867: Politics,
Newspapers, and the Union of British North America,* 2nd ed.
Toronto, ON: University of Toronto Press. 1965.

http://canadachannel.ca/HCO/index.php/3._The_Path_to_
Union_1864-67

http://epe.lac-bac.gc.ca/100/200/301/ic/can_digital_collec-
tions/charlottetown/index.html

JULY 1, 1867
The Boys' Book of School Stories. Toronto, ON: Blackie & Son.
(no date of publication but internal references seem to date
from the early 1930s)

http://history.cbc.ca/history/?MIval=EpContent.html&series_
id=1&episode_id=8&chapter_id=6&page_id=2&lang=E

http://www.imagescanada.ca/r1-250-e.html

LOUIS RIEL
Owram, D. "The Myth of Louis Riel." *Readings in Canadian History:
Post Confederation*, 3rd ed. Francis, R.D. and D.B. Smith (Eds.).
Toronto, ON: Holt, Rinehart and Winston of Canada, 1990.

http://en.wikipedia.org/wiki/Louis_riel

http://en.wikipedia.org/wiki/North-West_Rebellion

http://en.wikipedia.org/wiki/Red_River_Rebellion

THE INDIAN ACT
Berger, T.R. "Native History, Native Claims, and Self-
Determination." *Readings in Canadian History,* 3rd ed.

Berger, T.R. "Native History, Native Claims, and Self-
Determination." *Readings in Canadian History: Post
Confederation,* 4th ed. Francis, R.D and D.B. Smith (Eds.).
Toronto, ON: Harcourt Brace & Company, 1994.

http://en.wikipedia.org/wiki/Indian_Act

POUTINE ON THE NILE
MacLaren, R. *Canadians on the Nile, 1882–1898.* Vancouver, BC:
University of British Columbia Press, 1978.

When Laurier Met Diefenbaker
Wallechinsky, D., A. Wallace, I. Basen and J. Farrow. *The Book of Lists: The Original Compendium of Curious Information. The Canadian Edition.* Toronto, ON: Seal Books, 2005.

http://www.collectionscanada.gc.ca/primeministers/h4-3182-e.html

World War I
Papineau, T. "An Open Letter from Capt. Talbot Papineau to Mr. Henri Bourassa" and Bourassa, H. "Mr. Bourassa's Reply to Capt. Talbot Papineau's Letter." *Readings in Canadian History,* 3rd ed.

http://en.wikipedia.org/wiki/Canada_in_World_War_I

Prohibition, Income Tax and the Vote for Women
Moose Jaw: River of Many Turnings. Video Resource: 49th Parallel Productions, 1999.

http://en.wikipedia.org/wiki/Income_taxes_in_Canada

http://en.wikipedia.org/wiki/Nellie_McClung

http://en.wikipedia.org/wiki/Prohibition_in_Canada

http://en.wikipedia.org/wiki/Women%27s_suffrage#Canada

Tommy Douglas and Medicare
Margoshes, D. *Tommy Douglas: Building the New Society.* Montréal, QC: XYZ Publishing, 1999.

On to Ottawa
Struthers, J. "Canadian Unemployment Policy in the 1930s." *Readings in Canadian History,* 4th ed.

http://en.wikipedia.org/wiki/On_to_ottawa

http://www.thecanadianencyclopedia.com/index.cfm?PgNm=TCE&Params=A1ARTA0005926

WORLD WAR II AND AFTER

Prentice, A., P. Bourne, G. Cuthbert Brandt, et al. "The 'Bren Gun Girl' and the Housewife Heroine." *Readings in Canadian History*, 4th ed.

Gray, L. *Canada's World War II Aces: Heroic Pilots & Gunners of the Wartime Skies*. Edmonton, AB: Folklore Publishing, 2006.

http://en.wikipedia.org/wiki/Bren_gun_girl

http://en.wikipedia.org/wiki/DeHavilland_Mosquito

http://georgerout.com/radio.html

http://www.hamradio-online.com/1996/jan/hams.html

http://www.snopes.com/food/ingredient/carrots.asp

THE IMMIGRATION YEARS

http://www.pier21.ca/research/research-materials/the-first-seventy-five-years/#1

THE COLD WAR STARTS AT HOME

Whitaker, R. and S. Hewitt. *Canada and the Cold War*. Toronto, ON: James Lorimer and Company Ltd., Publishers, 2003.

http://en.wikipedia.org/wiki/Igor_Gouzenko

THE DIEFENBAKER GOVERNMENT SCRAPS THE AVRO ARROW

http://en.wikipedia.org/wiki/Avro_arrow

ON THE ROAD (TO THE DIEFENBUNKER)

http://en.wikipedia.org/wiki/Diefenbunker

Décharmé, M. *Straight From the Fridge, Dad: A Dictionary of Hipster Slang*. New York: Broadway Books, 2000.

Whitaker and Hewitt, *Canada and the Cold War*.

THE MUNSINGER AFFAIR
Whitaker and Hewitt, *Canada and the Cold War.*

1967: THE LAST GOOD YEAR
Marchand, P. *Marshall McLuhan: The Medium and the Messenger.*
Cambridge, MA: MIT Press, 1998.

http://www.youtube.com/watch?v=Orm-urRidH8

THE CANADARM
http://en.wikipedia.org/wiki/Canadarm

THE NATIONAL ENERGY PROGRAM
Le Riche, *Alberta's Oil Patch.*

THE GHOSTS OF STEPHEN HARPER: PAST, PRESENT AND FUTURE
http://en.wikipedia.org/wiki/Reach_for_the_Top

http://en.wikipedia.org/wiki/Stephen_Harper

Djordje Todorovic

DJORDJE TODOROVIC IS AN artist/illustrator living in Toronto, Ontario. He first moved to the city to go to York University to study fine arts. It was there that he got a taste for illustrating while working as the illustrator for his college paper, *Mondo Magazine*. He has since worked on various projects and continues to perfect his craft. Aside from his artistic work, Djordje devotes his time volunteering at the Print and Drawing Centre at the Art Gallery of Ontario. When he is not doing that, he is out trotting the globe. He has illustrated three other books.

Geordie Telfer

GEORDIE TELFER IS A WRITER, occasional playwright and sometime performer who lives in Toronto, Ontario. During a checkered but happily misspent youth, he was the assistant director for the Toronto Studio Players Theatre School, a freelance set carpenter and, on one occasion, the reluctant wrangler of a monkey and a ferret. Currently, he writes mainly for web and sometimes for television, having penned several documentaries airing on Discovery Canada and Animal Planet. He fills most of his days creating content for interactive projects associated with Treehouse TV, TVOKids and for other children's broadcasters across Canada. He is also the author of three other non-fiction titles, including *Real Canadian Pirates* and *A Dictionary of Canadianisms* also with Folklore Publishing.